Presented to:

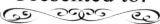

_____

From:

_____

Date:

_____

Endorsements

Imagine being in a terrible car accident that crippled and devastated you in body and spirit, resulting in over two decades of doctors, medicine, and surgery. Then imagine God allowing you to suffer terribly and not heal or help you—in spite of all your prayers. Then envision a moment that came in a special healing service in five minutes of being face-to-face with God. This happened for Pegge Golden. Pegge Golden tells her unbelievable story of suffering and healing, and of pain and grace. You must read every word to understand and believe what an awesome God both Pegge and you have. Will you have the courage to wait on God's will and calling as she did? Pegge's story is a must-read!

— Dr. Larry Keefauver
Bestselling Author and International Teacher www.doctorlarry.org

God took the pain Pegge walked through to birth a supernatural intimacy with Him, followed by a supernatural healing for her body, which gave birth to a supernatural ministry to others. May this book inspire you to let God do the same for you. Pegge discovered that God still speaks, God still delivers, and God still heals. May this book lead you into worship of our risen Savior.

— Dr. Mark Virkler
Founder, Communion with God Ministries

This is a true story, and I had the privilege of walking through some of this painful journey with Pegge when I was her Christian Leadership University professor. I can vouch for her pain; yet in spite of it, she was a serious, diligent student, constantly seeking God and completing her lessons with excellence beyond what was required.

Pegge has a heart for others and greatly desires to minister God's truth, goodness, mercy, love, and healing. If you need healing in any area of your life (spirit, soul, body, relationships, or lack of any kind), read Pegge's book. You will benefit through the knowledge she gained and become a victorious overcomer through Christ.

— Rev. Dr. Karen Joy King, Ph. D.
Christian Leadership University Professor, Pastor, New Beginnings Ministries of Fayette, Ohio

Awaken

Finding the Deep Well of Faith
for the Miraculous

An incredible 30-year journey
of healing against all odds

PEGGE GOLDEN

Printed in the United States of America.

ISBNs: 978-1-7376356-0-4 (Print)

978-1-7376356-1-1 (E-book)

Dedication

I want to dedicate my testimony to God. You have stretched my faith to believe all things are possible with You. You have shown me that You are much bigger than any problem I will ever face.

I want to thank my parents for raising me in the Lord, and also to thank my family and friends.

I pray for all who read this book to be touched by God and enter a new and deeper relationship with Him.

Thank you, dear Tanya Smirnova, for your support and guidance in editing and for your encouragement!

Table of Contents

Chapter 1: The Alarm Clock Was Ringing

Chapter 1: The Alarm Clock Was Ringing

I lay in my bed staring at the ceiling. How did I end up like this? A thirty-two-year-old successful businesswoman, diligent college student, sincere Christian motivated to succeed in all that God has promised me—and out of nowhere, my whole life changes! I wondered how many times I replayed the same scene over and over: I leave school and brake at the stop sign to see an old Crown Victoria come swerving over the hill and smash headfirst into the front of my car. The driver was doing sixty-five miles per hour. I remember the sound of metal roaring as my foot presses hard on the pedal. My little Toyota took the full impact as I screamed, "Jesus!"

My life would never be the same again. The accident had as much impact on my spiritual life as it did my physical because I believed God would protect me from this type of thing ever happening to me. I made my choice at a young age to live for God and prayed the prayer of salvation. I understood that the Spirit of God Himself came to dwell in me at that very moment, and from that point, His Spirit and my spirit were made one.

As I matured in my walk, God showed me from the Bible more of who He is and more of my identity in Him. I knew my soul and my body were in the process of being transformed into the likeness of God. I had considered my relationship with God as my greatest blessing. Every time I read the Bible, God was speaking into my life. He meant everything to me! I was determined to follow Jesus in all things as my example. I knew that God could never leave me or forsake me, yet with my own free will, I could choose to live eternally without Him. I read the promises that He made to me. He was always my choice! At least I thought He was.

As I sat totally crushed inside the car waiting for the first responders to rescue me, I was bewildered, and my mind was racing a million miles an hour looking for answers. "How could this happen to me?" I wondered. Until we go through something devastating, many of us are convinced that we are unstoppable! For me, life was going well, and I did not prepare for this!

As the human race, when we face pandemics, natural disasters, or severe weather, we get through it all together; but it is much more difficult to battle alone. This was true in my situation; just as the day I meet my Maker, it will be Him and I—this was personal. I had entered into a battle for my life, and the rules and regulations for this battle warred against my mind, flesh, and spirit. I was so used to running my life, but this would be a battle of "waiting on God," and in this waiting, I would have little or no control.

I am very thankful to God for all the prayers I prayed and all the lessons He taught me before the accident. Only God could prepare me for this battle, and only God could use this situation to show me what was truly in my heart. I could not see anything wrong with how I was living my life, which was my problem. A blind person knows that he or she is blind, but when a person with sight looks and all seems good in their eyes—they are in trouble. We have to depend on God's eyes to see from His perspective as He shows us our condition. All of humanity experiences trials and hardships, but spiritual battles exceed anything I could think or imagine. Let me explain.

What had I done wrong to deserve this?

After the accident, I could barely move my body. The doctors said I would be permanently disabled for the rest of my life! I knew I belonged to God, and I knew that He loved and cared for me. I was standing on His Word for healing, yet, deep down in my heart, I questioned, *What had I done wrong to deserve this?* Everything I had ever known about God, His principles, and my own beliefs were about to come on trial. My body was demanding proof of God's Word, and my spirit was clinging to Scriptures I memorized as a child. When I was hoping to be comforted with a Scripture, my mind would shout thoughts like, *Will*

I ever be able to get out of bed and walk? I continued fighting doubt as it lingered around me like a thick cloud. I could barely open my mouth, but I managed to ask God, "What am I supposed to do?"

The enemy was telling me loud and clear that this was God's plan for my life and that I needed to accept a lifetime of pain and disability, but I did not want to believe him! I would scream back from my broken heart, "Devil, I know God will heal me!" only to feel the pain searing through my body. Day after day, the pain of my body was colliding with the screeching thoughts of my soul. How would I ever be able even to hear the still small voice of God in my spirit from this war zone? I began to imagine what hell must be like—a place of agony and hopelessness. I knew that by Jesus' stripes, I am healed and that I remain under the protection of His Blood, yet this happened to me! What about the promise of abundant life and all that I was going to accomplish in my lifetime? How would I be able to fulfill all His promises to me in my present condition? I needed these questions answered, so I turned to my Bible because I knew only God's Word was the truth.

To be honest, I needed a miracle even to read the Bible! **If only I could move** with all the muscles ripped and torn some all three layers in my back; **if only I could sit** with my muscles torn in my lower spine; **if only I could read** with daily migraine headaches; **if only my arms could move** with torn shoulder muscles. The doctors told me I was only allowed to be in a sitting position no longer than twenty minutes. Discouraging? Yes, but my mind was fixed on the shock and awe that I survived this accident. Everything I had gone through before the accident taught me not to give up or quit. My fight was proof that God was not done with me yet! In this situation, my Father was expecting me to fight. And He did not leave me in this fight all by myself, for God's Word says God Himself fights my battles! I had to fight to trust Him and then rest in the knowledge that His wisdom would bring me understanding.

Life as I knew it was over, and my life after the accident was so new to me that I had to learn how to live in utter brokenness one day—and one limb—at a time. I was going to war with God for my healing! My strategy was to find the answers. So I prayed, *God, I am going to fight to read the Bible. Where should I start?* I would cry so hard because I never imagined that I would have to battle just to read the Good Book. My "first base" was to thank God that my parents took me to church growing up, where I heard the Word. The Bible that had become "optional" for me to read as an adult was now my life support.

God began answering my questions by training me visually through my soul. He helped me understand more about how He created me. God made Adam and Eve to be both physical and spiritual beings. I am a three-part being of spirit, soul, and body. My soul is my mind, will, and emotions, and like Adam, my soul had to choose to yield to God in the spirit or submit to the authority of the flesh. To me, it seemed so unfair because the agony in my flesh was dominating my character and the attitudes of my soul. For Adam and Eve, it was about not eating fruit in the garden of Eden, but to me, it was about my very life! Suddenly, I realized that our cases were similar. I had to fight to get to the Word, the Tree of Life, or my flesh would be in control, opening doors for the enemy. If my flesh became stronger than my soul, then my spiritual identity would lay dormant and be captive to the flesh. This was the "death" of Adam as he chose to live a natural and soulish life independent from God. But I am not Adam or Eve. "My name is Pegge Golden!" I cried, "and I have both the Blood of Jesus and the Holy Spirit!"

So what did my soul really believe?

All the pounding of the enemy on my flesh was an attempt to take my soul captive. I could see how my natural man was receiving wisdom from the flesh and the world through all the x-rays and reports. My spiritual wisdom was so broken that only the Holy Spirit could fix me! My spirit, soul, and body had to get our "free will" in agreement. I had to compare and choose between the two "wisdoms": the wisdom from my flesh or of God's Spirit. My flesh would rather die to be free from this agony, and my soul was almost agreeing with the flesh and debating all of this with me. So what did my soul really believe? I needed to examine, investigate, and inquire every question regarding every choice I ever made.

I knew that only the Holy Spirit understands the mind of God and man. So I asked Him to take me deeper into spiritual discernment and teach me how to recognize which spirit was speaking to me. There are three spirits involved.

There is the Spirit of God Himself, my spirit, and the spirit of the world, which is mingled with the voice of the enemy. I had to start testing, with the help of the Spirit, the very core of my thoughts: what I allowed to enter my mind, what I believed in, and why I do things the way I do. All of this was accomplished in the Word of God, but it would be weeks before I could pick the Bible up again. So how could this be accomplished? I had to keep reminding myself that God was with me, and He is the Word made flesh. I believed that Jesus knew everything I was going through because of what He suffered. He had me!

I would desperately try to remember the Word but could not. Thank God, He remembers it all! I was learning to depend on the Holy Spirit for my memory, and He would faithfully bring certain characters of the Bible to my remembrance. In my waiting, I could see how each person in the Old and New Testament represents each of us, and they absolutely represent Jesus! For example, in my mind, I could remember King David. What I remembered most about him is that he suffered intimately with God. Just like me, he cried out, "Why are You so far from helping me, and so far from the words of my groaning" (Psalm 22:1 NKJV). I knew that I had entered the intimacy of suffering that David spoke about. I knew God was so close to me, but my soul and flesh were travailing with anguish in the opposite direction. So I decided to do what King David did: be real with God. because my mouth could barely open, I spoke to Him from my heart, *"God, I know that nothing is hidden from You, because You know everything about me. I do not understand physical, mental, and spiritual suffering, but You do! Help me! Come closer to me."* And He did!

O my God, I cry in the daytime, but You answer
not; and by night I am not silent or find no rest.
(Psalm 22:2 AMPC)

Oh, how I related to David in this season! God anointed
him to be King of Israel—and everything went wrong since
the anointing. But David did not give up! He continued
alone in the quiet of his soul to trust God. He fixed his
gaze upon the Creator of the Universe, and still not much
changed for him. It became worse! Even the promises of
God seemed nonexistent in the physical realm, but David
knew that the spiritual realm held no limits. He blindly
believed what he heard in the secret place of prayer. God
sustained his life through so much hardship and rejection,
and I understood that this is where I had to walk with God.
There was nothing I could do to fix my body; I was literally
trapped. The only thing I could do is to go deeper into my
spirit with the Lord. I had to turn away from all the external
noises and turn inward to dwell in God's presence—even
when I couldn't pick up the Bible. In this place, alone and
with blind faith, I knew that God would sustain me. But
looking outward showed a whole different battle where the
opposite was seen.

Before the accident, I owned a farm, and I was blessed
to have faithful employees who could depend on me. Now
I was dependent on them. I would pray they would not
forget to come in and tell me all about their day. I began
to believe they no longer needed me and that my identity
as their boss was also slipping away. I started feeling that
I was more of a burden to people. At the same time, when
they came in to see me, I would groan inwardly. I wanted

my life back; my desire was to put this all behind me, start walking, and go back to work. Each time a worker came in, a different emotion would erupt within me as I would either feel sorry for myself or become more determined to fight this battle.

I truly enjoyed working the land. I had many animals, including a flock of sheep and a herd of goats. Like King David, I learned so much from them. I was the one who birthed them when assistance was needed, and if its mother rejected a lamb, I would bottle feed it. Each sheep had unique markings and personalities and its own name. I could tell the time of day by where the sheep were on the pasture; they were that predictable. As I lay down and remembered this, I wondered just how predictable I was to God. One thing I knew for sure was that sheep are totally defenseless. Now it was my turn to be totally reliant on the Good Shepherd. In the battle of "awakening," my life was no longer mine!

I was clueless about how I was to balance being reliant on God and yet a fighter. I was learning to be a disabled warrior, which in my mind made no sense. My soul felt robbed and violated. I was angry and fought against bitterness. The enemy would even use Scripture against me, trying to get me to believe his lies, just as he did with Adam and Eve. I was on a mission to fight against the loud voice of pain and press into the quiet voice of God. As I did, I couldn't resist reminding the devil that God gave me authority over every creeping thing and tell him to depart from me. God was within me, the devil tormented me, the world lied to me, and my own flesh wanted to give up and die. My soul was on the fence trying to remain still between my spirit and my crushed body while my heart ached for my body to move; I mumbled a roar, "It is finished, devil," and I could feel my flesh taunting me.

I was never going to give up on my healing because I had read the Book.

The Holy Spirit kept pointing me back to the life of Christ. Jesus is the ultimate example of dealing with trials and tribulations, with the world and the flesh warring within and around Him before, during, and after the crucifixion. No matter what Jesus faced, He found a way to remain firmly fixed on the will of the Father. This wasn't just something I wanted—I was in desperate need of this! Jesus knew His mission and fulfilled it. Would I complete the destiny God planned for me before the foundation of time with a broken and disabled body? I had to submit this to God—which almost killed me! Many believers become disabled and live a life submitted to God, and many are healed. If this was God's will, then I would drink from this cup, but I knew it wasn't. One thing was for sure: I was never going to give up on my full healing and restoration because I had read the Book.

What is a broken sheep expected to do in the presence of the All-Powerful God while waiting? Oh, the sheep learns that she has weapons! Let me explain: as a shepherdess, I had seen my sheep be attacked by dogs. The sheep were absolutely defenseless. They have no way of protecting themselves. When they were attacked, all they could do was bleat, thereby gaining my attention. Then I would grab my loaded shotgun and shoot over the dog's heads as I screamed death threats upon them, and they would run away. My sheep had to voice out their need to me so I could help them. My voice was given to me by God. Death and life are in the power of my tongue, and oh, how that devil would heat up the pain in my body, wanting me to speak evil over myself. The thoughts of pain and agony searing through my bones like fire showed me that he had no mercy. This was becoming a personal battle between us. I wanted to shoot bullets of Scripture at him from my mouth, but I couldn't remember them, yet in the deepest pain, I would remind him that God pulled me through another night. I would literally hear so quietly in my mind, *Did not God say that He would never give you more than you can handle?* And with all the faith I could muster at that time, I would reply, *Devil, the Shepherd and I will get through this together.* It was here that God released to me the spiritual weapon of prayer.

I had no idea how deep I would be trained in prayer! My body was taunting me to pray from my flesh, but this doesn't please God. My fleshly prayers were demanding and lifeless. The Holy Spirit wanted to train me to pray from the spirit. This took time—which I had plenty of. I did not see my prayers for myself answered immediately, so I dedicated my prayer time to others. I began interceding for every child to know the Word of God! From this altar of brokenness, I was learning to stop thinking about myself by praying for others. The more my thoughts or my body messed with me, the more I prayed. I was going to pray for others with sincerity to sow seeds into their lives—and I needed to reap a harvest of healing.

People have asked me to describe what the pain was like. The pain had no mercy, and I described it as one that was drowning. I have heard that when a person drowns, they see their life pass before them, and it is peaceful. Mine was different; I was under this tremendous weight of agony, and I could not get my footing. I could not move to swim or keep myself above water. Mine was not a quick death but long in suffering. I needed a breath in a body that could hardly hold air with the pain. In the hardest trial of my life, broken, ripped, crushed, and disabled, God's Holy breath was breathing truth for me. My soul, body, doctors, and the lies of the enemies bombarded me. I wondered, *How dysfunctional am I? How much does God actually care for me?*

How much do I care about Him?

There were times between surgeries when weeks would go by before I could get to the Bible again or even pray. In this season of constant agony, David and I were not the only ones who cried out to God. The Holy Spirit reminded me that Jesus Himself also cried out to His Father. Christ knew that the eyes of the Father were always upon Him, and this was how He remained in His perfect will. Jesus was never disconnected from His Father until He was on the cross covered in my sin, in mental torment with a broken body and wounded spirit. While hanging on the cross, Jesus cried out:

> My God, my God, why have you abandoned me? (Matthew 27:46 NLT)

Jesus cried out to our Father before me so I would never have to ask the question, "Why have You abandoned me?" This question was no longer possible because of Jesus' sacrifice, yet it was another reason I could say, "Thank You Jesus!" I began interceding for those who had not yet entered or understood suffering. This brought me so much comfort! Just like my Savior, I was looking up to heaven, praying for the body of Christ and expecting my healing. It was as if I set my spiritual camp right here in this place. I knew the gaze of the Father and Jesus was in perfect unity, but what about me? I saw their relationship! This was the union of unconditional love. Jesus surrendered completely to the Father. I understood that my life could no longer be mine if I wanted to have the same relationship with God as Jesus did. They were not separate. They were One as God, and I are one! You know, after looking up at the ceiling for so long, my eyes only found peace turning within to my spirit. I had enough of the flesh and the world! So I started following hard after God. I wanted to know everything about Him!

It was here where I pressed into union through a relationship with God and asked Him to show me how I can remain in this dwelling place. I started learning what it meant to "abide" in Him, to live with Him, to move and breathe in Him in a world that had no sin, no sickness, no pain, and no death from within a body and soul on fire in pain and brokenness. I understood the world still has plagues, sickness, death, and disease because of the works of the enemy and rebellious disobedience by mankind to God and His Word. It was in this secret place, the kingdom of heaven within me, that I found true freedom. The prophetic words of Jesus' promises collided with my soul and body. Heaven was alive within me. Jesus said He was my refuge and strong tower. Could there be a place of peace within a screaming body?

> For God alone my soul waits in silence; from Him comes my salvation. He alone is my rock and my salvation, my defense and my strong tower; I will not be shaken or disheartened. (Psalm 62:1-2 AMPC)

The promises of God were becoming more than just words on a paper—they were alive! I was so humbled to see the real me, and I cried out to God in repentance. I honestly thought I loved God so much, but I never realized all I was missing! It wasn't that my life caused God to move away from me; I had allowed life to move me away from my Father. The Holy Spirit showed me that I was missing out on so much love and relationship with my Creator through my control of self. God's love was flowing in me like a raging river. My constant time in His presence began taking over my life in ways I never thought or could have imagined. It was only through experiencing each Scripture come alive that I could truly see!

The Alarm Clock Was Ringing

In my brokenness, I became His mission, and now He alone has become mine. If Jesus needed quiet time with His Father, so did I. Why was all of this not important to me before the accident? God was judging my pain. The Holy Spirit revealed the truth. My alarm clock was ringing, and in the hardest trial of my life. I was living in a place of encountering His unconditional love. Here the question became, "How much do I care about Him?" The experience was more foreign to me than the pain. I wanted Him more than my healing!

My whole life was changed instantly through a horrible accident, but the eyes of my soul looked into the depths of the Word made flesh! This was the Holy Spirit taking me deeper into Christ, and I was moving with the Shepherd in a body that could barely function. It was no longer me waiting for God to take care of everything; it was the Holy Spirit and I doing life together as He did with Jesus! I was determined to journal my days and nights with Him. The more I wrote, the more He gave me! The Holy Spirit was developing my spiritual hearing.

Prayer:

Father God, I want to learn how I can relate with You NOW as Jesus related with You in unity while He was still in the flesh! I know this is available to me because Jesus did this while He was alive on the earth! Thank You for Your beautiful Holy Spirit!

God, how did I value my life as more important than You? How could I be so blind that I thought I saw perfectly? Teach me, Holy Spirit, to receive all that Jesus has provided for me. I find so much comfort in knowing that Jesus is still praying for me. I am depending on You to uncover my "blind spots." What else am I blind to that I don't even know I can't see? Thank You for the kingdom of heaven within me! Thank You that You are real and Your Word is True! Thank You, God, in Jesus' name, amen.

Prayer Points

Are you praying for your tomorrow and your future, asking God to prepare you for all you will need?

Do you have enough Word within your heart to war through a battle?

What would you do if something like this happened to you or someone you love?

Who does your soul side more with: your spirit (obeying God's Word) or your flesh (spending more time doing what (self) wants?

Ask yourself: are you doing life with God, or are you letting God come along with you?

Chapter 2: Does God Care?

Chapter 2: Does God Care?

I remembered how alert I was during the accident, and now it seems like I memorized even the smallest details. I never lost consciousness. I remember how the first responders struggled to keep me calm until they could get me out of the car. Even after they shut the ambulance doors, to my surprise, I didn't see much blood. My mind was still aware enough to tell them that we couldn't leave for the hospital until they brought my books from the car because I had to study for an exam.

Even lying in the emergency room, I thought I had control of the situation and believed this would be over soon. I could see the drivers standing outside the door of my room talking with the nurse. I was trying to hear what they were saying, but I couldn't because my mind was processing and full of questions, like, "Why didn't God warn me about this accident?" I knew it would have been easy for Him to lead me home in a different direction or tell me not to attend classes that day. How will I fulfill the destiny You promised me—a life of abundance?

Awaken

That Friday evening, the emergency room was packed. I remember my doctor flying around, popping in and out of my room. They did some quick tests, and the doctor said that my muscles would be sore for a couple of weeks and that I would need to follow up with my family doctor. He said he had a flight to catch and hoped I would feel better! The nurses made the follow-up appointment with my doctor for Monday, and then I was released. They gave me a package of muscle relaxers and called my friend's husband to pick me up. Before I left, the ambulance driver peeked in to ask me if I still thought George Washington was the president of the United States. I tried to smile and thank him for his kindness, wondering if I had actually said that. I remember thanking God for saving my life.

As I lay in the back seat of the car, I remember how my friend's husband looked at me—scared! I had no idea what I looked like, so I told him I would be okay. I couldn't open my mouth, so I was mumbling! I remember him telling me not to worry and that they would get me a rental car and drop it off for Monday's appointment. I was grateful! As he pulled me by my feet to get me out of the car, I remembered telling him to leave the rental in the yard. I told him I had food and was going to rest. Again, I thought everything was under control. I called my mom to tell her about the accident and what the doctor had said. I asked her to let everyone know because I had a hard time talking and wanted to lie down. I promised to call her after my follow-up appointment with the doctor on Monday.

Next, I looked in the mirror and saw the swelling and black and blues on my face. As I undressed, I could see the mark of the seatbelt on my stomach and chest. As I got in my pajamas, I could see blood on my left foot, and my right foot had the mark of my brake pedal. All I heard in my mind was Psalm 91, "Because I have made the Lord, who is my refuge, even the Most High, my dwelling place, no evil shall befall me....and He will give His angels charge over me in all my ways so I will not dash my foot against the stone."

Why didn't God warn me about this accident?

I remained on the couch as my heart was thanking God for never leaving me. I remember being so stiff I could hardly move. I had to concentrate on something else and started remembering how many times God faithfully saved me, and with these thoughts, I fell asleep. When I had to get up to use the restroom, the pain worsened, and I thought something had to be wrong. I kept encouraging myself that the pain would soon be over and that my muscles were just sore. To be honest, I made it through that Friday night by the grace of God! By Saturday morning, I knew I had to stop drinking as much water with the muscle relaxers because of how hard it was to get up to go to the restroom. The pain was stronger, affecting my ability to think clearly, yet there was also more numbness. On my way back to the couch, I unlocked the kitchen door in case the ambulance drivers had to get back in to help me. I kept reminding myself that God was with me! By Sunday, the pain was so intense I was losing reality, yet I kept reminding myself what the doctor told me. After all, he was someone with knowledge in this area. I received his diagnosis and I had to take his word because this was all new to me.

Monday afternoon, I made it down the three stairs to the car to get to my doctor. To this day I don't know how, but I drove there! I cannot tell you how long it took me to get in and out of that car. When my doctor looked at me, his face changed, and I saw fear in his eyes. He could not believe I had driven to this appointment! He gave me a shot and had me brought back to the hospital, where scans showed my body was "crushed." I had to have appointments with specialists who told me there was a good possibility I might never walk again. Fear was truly trying to grab me, and I replied to each doctor that they did not know "Who my God is!" But to be honest, I wanted to believe the report of the first doctor!

The top of the steering wheel had crushed my face. The Myofascial surgeon, who was about to retire, said that in his entire career, he had never seen a face as damaged as mine. They had to see which nerves were alive and to test this, fifty needles were inserted on each side of my face with an electrical charge put through them to see if my muscles could contract. The surgery was horrific, and the pain after was unimaginable. I used to say that I thought an ear or toothache was the worst pain ever. The whole face was in extreme pain, almost beyond what I could bear. Even after the surgery, my mouth could not open. My surgeon told me that if it wasn't for the gap in my front teeth, he probably would have removed one of them so I could take in fluids by mouth. I could not eat, and over the next few months I lost forty pounds. Six months later, my mouth could open the width of one finger.

The following year I was told that I would need the same procedure done again. My mouth was not opening, and the pain in my face was unrelenting; this didn't even take into account the rest of my body. In my heart, I was so mad at God, but in my mind, I was still thankful! I used to love singing praise to God, and now even that was stolen from me. For the next twenty-five years, it was rare for my mouth to open even for a natural yawn. But more than anything, I wanted to understand why this accident happened to me because my spirit was at war with my soul, trying to find something to comfort my body.

I had read the Gospels, and I pictured myself walking with Jesus as He did His many miracles. It was wonderful and exciting! But this time, I noticed the hardship and suffering of the people and also of Jesus Himself. A Scripture came to my remembrance:

> Jesus wept. So the Jews were saying, See how He loved him [as a close friend]! But some of them said, Could not this Man, who opened the blind man's eyes, have kept this man from dying?" (John 11:35-37)

I noted how He was treated, how He suffered, and how He pressed on. I was suffering too! I was in so much pain that my teeth were being ground down by the pressure of my biting to withstand the pain. Through my pain, I was learning that the Holy Spirit was not only given to me to have a wonder-filled emotional party full of goosebumps and laughter, which is great, but a place where He would pull me free from myself and bring me back into the heart of the Father.

God's emotions and my emotions were about to collide!

The days were long, and the nights were longer. The dark cloud of doubt surrounded me. The more I tried to focus on God, the more I was being drawn deeper into His character. It was back then when I discovered a great truth: God has emotions! He has many attributes, and I, as a person created in His image, have many attributes. But here, God's emotions and my emotions were about to collide! My emotions were waging war within my soul against being so humbled and helpless. I knew I couldn't hide them from God; His eyes were upon me, and I was full of unrighteous anger and self misery! I saw a side of myself I didn't know existed. This real me wanted answers, and I wanted accountability. The real me had no intention of backing down, but neither did God! One day the Holy Spirit reminded me of Jacob.

Jacob had just received all the inheritance of his father, Isaac. His father, who could not see well, wanted to give the blessing to the oldest son (The story of Jacob can be found in Genesis 27-35). Rebecca, Isaac's wife, knew the younger was to receive this blessing because God told her when she carried the twins in her womb that the older would serve the younger. Jacob received the blessing, and instead of throwing a huge party, he had to flee. The blessing he received pushed him out of his comfort zone, removed what he knew, and led him to dwell in a land he knew not, with family members he barely knew! His story really spoke to me. Many hard and fruit-filled years later, God instructed Jacob to return home. Yet even on the way home, he had no control of what would happen. The Bible tells us that he wrestled with a "man." Some say he wrestled with God, and some say an angel. I wondered how he could wrestle with either and be in a winning position. Now I understood Jacob: with all the anguish of my spirit, soul, and body, I felt I was wrestling in a spiritual battle. I was not letting go until God blessed me.

I read the promises and was not backing down! Jacob received a disability in his hip and a name change from Jacob (the trickster) to "Israel." Well, life was still hard for him—even in the blessing, but he believed God for his provision and protection. I was like Jacob; I was going to push through and not let go, not going to be alive in a dead body. Unity was about to happen in God and my emotional relationship. It was in my brokenness when God revealed to me His great emotion—love! Love was the absolute furthest thing from what I was experiencing. My knowledge of love was so distanced from Him, who is Love. Love is the nature of God, and He wanted me to feel as He feels, to reflect our love for each other. But I did not understand how there can be love in pain and torment? So I asked, "God, by Your grace, You have allowed me to live through the crushing of my body, the anguish of my soul, and the death of my heart's desires. Is this not enough that now even my eternal soul seems to be on trial?" I knew that my spiritual soul is my character, motives, emotions, attitudes, my will, my choice, and my attributes. It's what lives with me through eternity! And that list has to be transformed into looking like God. I honestly wondered how much more God thought I could handle! But I am created in His image, and He wanted to show me where I was reflecting Him in my walk and where I was not. This astounded me!

I received understanding by seeing how much God suffered for me!

My Father is holy, just, good, eternal, infinite, unchangeable, merciful, and truthful! He is gentle, kind, joyful, loving, peace-filled, faithful, full of wisdom, knowledge, understanding, and unlimited in everything! Let me not forget His patience and long-suffering! I received understanding by seeing how much God suffered for me! The Holy Spirit allowed me to see how people suffer and even how creation suffers. I repented. God wants us to be united through this suffering so we could minister to one another. No matter how ugly I acted and what was lacking through pain, God chose to minister to me. I would never have imagined God ministering to me, but not only did He minister to me day by day, but God also wanted me to minister to Him. I had read about the many mysteries of Christ but I entered by His grace into the mystery of suffering.

I went from a place of raging against bitterness to a cleansing of my spiritual soul as I realized how this mystery worked. **Why did I think of God as the All-Powerful Who would stop my suffering when He knows more about suffering than I ever will?** I was experiencing the attributes of God and how He felt the sorrow and victory, and this was bringing me comfort. You may question if God can feel sorrow because He is in heaven and there is no sorrow in heaven, but God is everywhere, including living inside of our mortal bodies. I had plenty of time to reflect on the truth of how I experienced happiness, anger, pain, loneliness, and sorrow and compare it to Jesus' soul. I reflected a lot of my unhappy emotions, but I was not reflecting the love He shared with me through these emotions.

To be honest, the way I thought, loved, and acted was broken, and this had nothing to do with the accident. Without my love in union with His, I could not love Him as Jesus loves Him. I was not allowing His love to penetrate my heart that had known so much hurt, and I needed to open to Him so His love could flow through me to others. Everything the world showed me as love I thought was acceptable, but it was just a superficial mirror that lied to me. I was deceived. I needed to love *with* Christ, not separate from Him. I knew I carried Christ to the world as I ministered to others throughout my life, but I wanted to see what others would see when I ministered to them. Was it God or just broken me? Only the Holy Spirit knew where I saw dimly, and I submitted to His cleansing. I needed a total transformation!

I found myself venting to God about how bad I struggled in many areas and how ignorant I was for not taking my spiritual life more seriously. There is nothing more important than my eternal soul, and God was listening and watching me intently. I did not obey Him, nor did I take His Word seriously. I considered spending time in our relationship to be optional, yet I thought we had a great relationship! My actions placed a block in our covenant. Not only did I treat God wrong, but I could see how this affected me and all those around me. Jesus was so kind to me, but I did not return His kindness. I could glimpse His unconditional love for me enough to see how I returned my love to Him. And I did all of this while I daily professed how much I loved Him! I think the worst sin I ever committed was ignoring Him, who daily loved me with all that He is without condition. I used to sing, telling God I wanted to love Him with my whole heart, soul, mind, and strength, and I honestly thought I was doing it. Oh, how blind I was! I wondered why it was hard for me even to receive His love many times, and I finally understood why! It was me; I didn't show up.

Imagine lying totally broken from your head to your feet, not having control of your soul and mind, and facing the real you—who you never thought you had to face—and yet God had no intention of giving up on me or condemning me or even looking down on me. In my place of brokenness, God could no longer be just a religion but a Person. He patiently taught me to love myself with His love because He was the only One capable of loving me. In this place of intimacy, I gave Him my true allegiance. I found my worth in His suffering for me! I could no longer be conformed to this world. I had to be transformed by the renewing of my mind (Romans 12:1-2). How many times have we read these words in the Bible and the result brought little change? These are not words—they are Him!

Because of His love and His suffering, I was able to bring myself daily to Him as a living sacrifice just as I was (Romans 12:1). What freedom I received! I began seeing my broken, pride-filled, and bossy self through His eyes: holy, beloved, and well-pleasing while coming into agreement with the perfect will of God where I was letting it go. All the while, He knew that I still blamed Him for the accident! I believed He would keep me from the little things if I was "good." I went to church and paid my tithe most of the time. Was this what I really thought a relationship with God would be like? At my worst, I met the infinite, inexplicable love of God for His creation. I blamed everyone and everything else without being able to see the different reflection between us. I embraced the cross and repented! I needed to understand the importance of how God leads me on the path as my Shepherd.

> When I was a child, I spoke as a child, I understood as a child, I thought as a child; but when I became a man, I put away childish things. For now we see in a mirror, dimly, but then face to face. Now I know in part, but then I shall know just as I am also known. And now abide faith, hope, love, these three; but the greatest of these is love. (1 Corinthians 13:11-13 NKJV)

Which report are you going to believe?

The life I once knew was behind me. My family and friends faded because they did not like seeing me like this.

I could barely make it to the church! I went from being wealthy to having to spend all my savings because the other driver had no insurance, and my medical policy was nowhere close to what I needed if a catastrophe struck. When all the resources I had were gone, I would have to live on disability. I had none of the control that I thought I had. The world, the enemy, my broken life were screaming, "Which report are you going to believe?" The doctors said I would remain the way I was on painkillers for the rest of my life. They gave me their report in writing. The enemy declared victory; he thought that all the prophetic words over me and all that God had gifted me with was "asleep." And at the same time, God showed me what was really stealing, killing, and destroying my eternal life with God right now. I had to turn back to God with my own free will as there could be no strain between us. He didn't want me to be away from Him any longer!

> Therefore He says, Awake, O sleeper, and arise from the dead, and Christ shall shine (make day dawn) upon you and give you light. Look carefully then how you walk! Live purposefully and worthily and accurately, not as the unwise and witless, but as wise (sensitive, intelligent people), making the very most of the time [buying up each opportunity], because the days are evil. Therefore, do not be vague and thoughtless and foolish, but understanding and firmly grasping what the will of the Lord is. (Ephesians 5:14-17 AMPC)

Prayer:

Father, I did not understand how close You are to me or how much You care for me! I am so sorry for ignoring the God of all creation who allows me to call You Father! I am now rejoicing because even with everything broken, we united in a depth I never knew was possible! I want to go through my life with You as Jesus did, and not apart from You as Adam and Eve. Teach me, Holy Spirit, how I can minister to You through prayer, fasting, worship, and time in the quiet! Teach me how to be in union with You all the time. I am so abundantly blessed to belong to You! Thank You for forgiving me. Thank You for putting me back on the path by uncovering what was stolen from me. Thank You for showing me that Jesus truly is the Word made flesh. Thank you that Your love found me in my absolute worst place. Thank You that You cared! I cannot ever feel unworthy again. I am so much more than flesh in this mundane world. Thank You for revealing these truths to me!

Prayer Points

Who knows more about being humbled and dependent on God than Jesus? When we understand that God cares we don't have to hide anything about ourselves from Him.

"What report will you believe?" Will it be what someone is gossiping about you, a doctors' report, or even low self-esteem found within yourself. Our answer is always found in Jesus Christ, our example in all things.

How do you honestly feel when you are ignored? Maybe we can use these emotions as a reminder to go spend time with God.

Is your eternal life a priority that you are growing in everyday NOW from earth?

God speaks of His love for us throughout the Bible and our lives. Get quiet with the Lord and let Him know how you feel about Him.

Chapter 3:
Relationship with Sin

Chapter 3: Relationship with Sin

Why did this happen to me? I knew that there would be trials and tribulations in the life of a believer, but this question kept rising from the depths within me. I knew God was with me, protected me, and kept me alive, yet I sensed there was so much more to this question. What was I not seeing or understanding? What did God want me to see? **What was my part in all of this?** Did I sin and open doors to the enemy? These were my thoughts as I was in the prep room for another surgery, and I found myself looking back through my life.

Now I realized that I was not as close in the relationship with God as I had once thought and could see how many other things had gone wrong. I truly expected the abundant life Jesus died for me to have right here on earth, but now I could also see how quickly I had settled for less than the abundant life. I had listened to so many preachers who said every promise from God was "Yes and Amen," and this is true, but I was tangled in man's doctrines, and this was very scary! The promises of God are for those who obey as well as those that do not. I had so much to learn—and I did not want to be cut open again! I wanted a miracle. I wanted to know how to make the healing Jesus provided for me manifest in my body right NOW! No one else had my answers except the Holy Spirit!

In reality, the muscles on the right side of my neck had atrophied and had to be removed. Also, if I turned my neck in a certain position, it was hard to take in a breath. I thought losing my breath was from the pain, but it was also from compression. These muscles were "crushed" from the impact, and they were shrinking. After the surgery and even with rehabilitation, my head hung on my shoulder, and I was truly suffering from migraine headaches almost daily. I thought the steering wheel that crushed my face was what kept my head on my shoulders. Doctors said I would remain this way. There was no word I could use to describe the pain of my body or what was happening in my mind. All of these nerve bundles going down my neck once were knit together by God, and now man was messing around inside of me. I began to wonder how my heart could continue beating with so great a daily trauma. And yet, I am the miracle who carries the miracle-working power of God within me. This was my "faith" reminder, as only His grace was keeping me alive. I had to trust God without understanding!

My doctors had the schedule for surgeries lined up for the next year. The following year they needed to take out my first rib on my right side. Usually, doctors will remove a rib from the neck or shoulder area, but in my case, they made a five-inch incision under my arm to remove it. Can you imagine someone cutting a huge gap under your arm and reaching in to rip out a rib? I whined worse than Israel ever did. **What was God's**

purpose through all of this? I wrestled with God using Scripture, saying, "God, You took a rib out of Adam to make Eve, and now they are taking out the rib! Please, God, just tell me what to do to be healed, and I will obey You this time!"

I couldn't get comfortable at all. If I did fall asleep, it wasn't long until I breathed wrong or had a muscle spasm, and the pain woke me. The worst part was that I could not simply sit down and relax; my muscles were not able to do that. Instead, the muscle spasms would sometimes leave me black and blue. My arms and my legs would thrash so badly in the bed that I asked God if I was demon-possessed. I was mean and miserable and honestly do not know how God could even stand me. To be honest, I would not want to be my friend, but God loved me just as I was. **The pain exposed the real me! The pain showed me all that was hidden that I was never able to see.** I had no idea how much sin, trauma, and wounds were within me. I had been taking my relationship with God as a suggestion. I had no idea who I even was anymore.

I wondered why I wasn't praying more seriously about my future, and if I had, would this accident have been prevented? When life was easier, I didn't pray as much as I should have, and this was a lesson I could not afford to forget. I attended church and read my Bible, and I brought God along with me as I did life. Certainly, He did not want this to happen to me, but I was not walking in agreement with Him. I knew that God had great plans for my future; He had thoughts of peace and not evil. Was He trying to tell me not to go to school that day, and I wasn't listening? The truth was that the life I said I gave to Christ was still in my control, and I handled it the best I knew how. My life was full of error, and this left me deceived. I was surrounded by God but thought my way of doing things was right. My way was the free will that God gave me (just being honest), and there were far too many "I's" in a relationship where there is only one God, and that should not have been me being in charge.

God was patiently waiting on me to open my eyes, to share His love with me every morning, but I would grab my phone instead or complain about my pain. I did my own thing while in the presence of God, and this was sin for me. Yes, sin because God was not in first place, and even still, God kept encouraging me and telling me to keep believing in Him. I murmured and complained, thinking that I was "yielding." **I wanted God to do things my way. I wanted God to heal me my way.** Sin sat between God's perfect will and plan for my life and my perfect will and vision of my relationship with God. I was waiting on God to heal me, and God was waiting on me to relate and cooperate with Him!

When it came to repenting, I was not maturing. The word *repent* would make me think about the Ten Commandments: did I lie, steal, cheat, covet, or commit adultery? I was to have no other god before Him—especially pride! I did not realize that sin is not just a list but a covering. Sin's purpose is to put distance between God and us. Sin is like a veil that covers our "blind spots." These blind spots make us think more like the enemy than our Father, but we don't see it, hence the word *blind*. The purpose of sin is to stop believers from reflecting God in this world. As a believer, I can repent for my sins, but I do not repent for what I do not see. The enemy is determined to cover our relationship with God. In this world, which desperately needs the Lord, there is a great harvest. Sin takes our focus from God to waste time and keep us from knowing who we are in Christ, to make us ashamed to spread the good news to the perishing world. We do not just get saved to go with God; we "grow" with God. This is the daily abiding relationship that we need with our heavenly Father, but the enemy wants us to go with him instead.

As the Holy Spirit opened my eyes, I saw sin as a war that this believer did not know how to fight. I was never supposed to fight this war alone, and the Holy Spirit was here to give me an understanding of how sin operates. Sin was now everything that I do not agree with God on. Backsliding is taking a step back from the Lord, and on a narrow path, that can never be good. I was being taught how much power there is in agreement, but I had to see without blinders who I agreed with. **Was the covered deception inside of me agreeing with the wicked ways of the world?** I needed the Holy Spirit to bring revelation to me about repentance so that I could mature. I was taught cycles and patterns as the Holy Spirit took me through the Bible just focusing on sin and its effects. There is a way out; as believers we can repent, but we need to know how sin operates and how it affects our souls. Did you know that there are generational sins? For example, generational sickness travels from great-grandpa to great-grandson. Generational sins even affect our love lives, bringing divorce or children born outside of the marriage covenant. The Bible is full of cycles and patterns, and this is why we have to diligently seek the Word of God with the Holy Spirit. With understanding, we can see where we have struggled even in our ancestor's footsteps and repent. There are also many generational blessings. I wanted to find the generational blessings so I could pray deeply for them to continue. For example, the blessings of Abraham are mine that I may receive the promise of the Spirit through faith for my children and their children (Galatians 3:14).

Many of us feel the weight of sin through family dysfunction and live with its effects, almost believing this is "normal." Children and adults grow wounded and go throughout life seeking relief, and since deliverance is not really accepted in the church, people are left in bondage. We see all the problems and horrible things happening in the world today as it happened in the Bible. Atonement is God saving us through the Spirit with life in the Word, keeping us free. Sin wants us to accept less, to see our life as mundane and perhaps with only a little of the power of God dwelling in our churches and lives. Sin pushes a perspective of receiving all that Jesus atoned for when we get to heaven, and not so much while on earth, but this is not Scriptural. As a believer, I am a supernatural being having a brief human experience.

Had I become numb to the truth? The Word states that those who lie will not enter the kingdom of heaven. God is everywhere, so as a believer, when I lie to a person, I am also lying in the face of God who dwells in me. When I believe a lie, it will also affect me. The world portrays that a little lie really doesn't hurt anybody, but it does. If I don't repent of the lie, its seed would grow, actually become contagious and causing me to lie more and more, thinking it was no big deal. It would wound my soul. Jesus did not want me to be misled or deceived, as seed time and harvest time remain. Lies hurt everyone and we can see this throughout all of history, but I needed the Holy Spirit to help me understand sin and my relationship with it. When I could actually see this truth, I no longer wanted to lie at all because I understood how this sin operated. I believe the moment I got saved I was supposed to start learning how to behave on earth as I will in heaven. No one lies in heaven. As I repented, God's love was there to free me with understanding, healing my soul. Jesus overcame this sin, and through repentance with understanding I experienced His true freedom.

All throughout the Bible, I read where both believers and unbelievers through the generations took sinning against God as optional. Now I can see how sin steals from me, from my relationship with God, from my generation—and if I do not understand that sin has a life of its own, it will continue. I never want to hide with sin again. The Word says that if possible even the elect will be deceived. I have to be under the daily training of the Holy Spirit, yet the Holy Spirit led me back to my example—Jesus.

Jesus began His ministry by getting baptized by John the Baptist in the Jordan River. The Holy Spirit comes down to Him in the form of a dove, and the voice of the Father is heard saying, "This is My Beloved Son in whom I AM well pleased." Directly after this amazing experience, Jesus is led into the wilderness for a very long fast (Matthew 3:13). Again, there was no celebration and no phenomenal miracle, sign, or wonder. Instead, we read that Jesus was led up by the Spirit into the wilderness to be tempted by the devil" (Matthew 4). Well, if Jesus can be tempted by the enemy, I certainly need to pay close attention to how He handles it! Did Jesus know He would be tempted? I have to say yes because the devil doesn't do anything new. Jesus knew we would be tempted by him, and He showed me by His example how to deal with the devil and temptation; with prayer, fasting, and by speaking the very same words He did. He is the Word, and He spoke the Word.

But again, there is so much more! How many times have we rebuked the devil and saw nothing change? Jesus, my example, showed me He defeated the enemy not only with the Word but also the power of God present in the Holy Spirit living within Him and us. Every example of Jesus throughout the Old and New Testament is for us to learn how to follow Him.

The Bible tells us clearly about sin and the effects of disobedience. Even though I read it and declared that I gave my life to Jesus, I was still sinning. I had everything that I needed: His Word, His Blood, and especially the Holy Spirit, but sin remained optional. I believed that if I sinned, I just had to say I was sorry. What I did not realize was that sin is a living substance that has its own way of operating, and it would keep repeating itself until I took it seriously. Sin is overcome by surrender, but we think we already have surrendered, and when we gave our lives to Jesus that "It was finished." Sin had me snared because I was in agreement with it. Jesus had nothing in common with sin but I surely did. Sinning is not normal but a chain to create distance in my relationship with God. It was preventing me from receiving all that Jesus' sacrifice entitled me. Sin covers all like a blanket comforting us in the dark as it keeps us asleep and it covers our families, churches, government, and nations.

They say that when you see an iceberg, you only see a small percentage of it and that the majority of the iceberg is hidden under the surface of the water. My question of "What was my part in all of this" revealed much more than I expected. It wasn't until the tormenting and relentless pain from this accident that I could see what was at the bottom of my iceberg. Under the surface was much more than I knew about myself, both negative and positive. There were patterns I did without knowing why I did things that way. Above the surface, I was a very loving and caring person, and I showed others how to walk as a Christian. I wanted to do this in excellence for God, but if you pushed my buttons, I could be very ugly. Who was I kidding? Certainly not God! Yet, in my heart, I wanted God to mean everything to me! He knows everything hidden in the heart of man, and this knowledge of sin woke me from a deep sleep. Then the Holy Spirit started teaching me to guard against spiritual deception that would allow sin to abide in my soul and body. He made me aware of Satan's strategies, and this knowledge of him and my own hidden self left me very weak. I would overcome only as I constantly depended on the Lord. I absolutely loved God, but there was a mixture in me that I did not understand.

God speaks about a mixture in the Bible. He chose a people—a nation—and delivered them from slavery. God sent them to go into a land He promised and commanded the Israelites to destroy all the "mixture" that would pollute His chosen people. These were spiritual practices of evil that the other nations worshipped. When God's people obeyed Him, they would win every battle, yet after a while, they would "drift" away from God and rebel. Then they would cry out to the Lord, as I did, and He would come and rescue them. Then they would repeat the same cycle of rebelling, repenting, and crying—but in all of this, sin is the common denominator.

God knew that if the foreign lands with their foreign gods were not destroyed completely, that they would mix with the chosen people and infect them. The thing about our God is that He walked with the nation of Israel, and He walks with each of us. I cannot sin without God knowing, and I no longer want to say I am sorry for lying just because I got caught. This is repentance when God and I see sin together, and together we close its door—and keep it closed!

When I repent with God, all I can see is the depths of my being in His goodness and kindness growing within me. Here I see myself with His eyes, and His love overwhelms me. I had no idea how much spiritual sin weighs, but I now understand why He wants me to cast aside every weight (Hebrews 12:1). On top of all my suffering, the substance of sin was where God chose to begin my healing. My physical body could not handle any more trauma, and my spirit needed my soul whole.

God began training me in discernment, to test the spirits, and to rightly divide His Word. Repentance is a believer's lifestyle and a great part of any relationship. I used to blame the enemy for everything, which also was a trap to keep me from looking at myself. Now I can look and deal with my own actions with God who sees all. Repentance allows intimacy to overtake the strain and bring healing with knowledge. My spiritual life was truly being transformed. I remember a client who told me that he never had to tell God that he was sorry again because he said it at the prayer of salvation. I am accountable to God for every single breath of our relationship. I could not imagine a relationship where there is no relating.

There is also the other side of "mixture" where people believe that they have sinned so badly there is no way they could be forgiven. Without allowing the Word of God and the Holy Spirit to guide us just as He did Jesus, these mixtures lead to traps both demonic and in doctrines made by man.

Relationship with Sin

Sin is seed! Sin covers more than the person who commits it but all who are affected by it. Let's observe how the apostles followed Jesus. They loved Him. They said they would die with Him, but we saw they ran in the garden of Gethsemane. The apostles watched all the miracles, signs, and wonders, but it did not change them. They still had issues just like me! Jesus was external for them. He lived on the outside of them, and when Jesus died, they were still seeking answers. Their lives didn't change until they obeyed Him and prayed, waiting on the Holy Spirit. Everything changed when the apostles received the Holy Spirit inside of them, and the power and presence of God once again became evident on the earth. Jesus said He would not leave us "orphans" because we are His family! An orphan is a picture of me trying to do all of this on my own and I was beating myself up for failing.

This is why I love the question that Paul asked in Acts 19:2, "Did you receive the Holy Spirit when you believed?" My relationship with God is real, and the enemy is real, but only I am accountable when I stand before God. I can only depend on the counsel of God to keep me on the straight and narrow path. I cannot see where I am blind, but I want to judge myself now with the revelation of the Holy Spirit creating a clean heart in me and renewing a contrite spirit. I want the Holy Spirit to overtake my life because my eternal life has already begun and I cannot bear living in pain and torment. My relationship with sin used my wounds to drift me toward the pain and away from my Solution—Jesus!

Prayer:

If you have never asked Jesus to be the Lord and Savior of your life, let today be your choice to begin a life spent eternally with the One true God who loves you! Even if you are unable to receive His love, let Him find the way into your heart:

Father, I thank You for sending Jesus to come in the flesh as God and man to dwell with us, to relate with us, to die for us, and to shed His Blood to pay the price for my sin. I thank You, Father, that as Jesus was raised from the dead, the veil of the temple was torn, removing all that got in the way of our relationship. Jesus, I believe You died for me, shed Your Blood on the cross, and resurrected to prepare a place for me, and if all that wasn't enough, You pray for me day and night. I am sorry for allowing sin to strain our relationship. Wash me clean with Your precious Blood. Free me from the sins of my ancestors and any curses that I am continuing on in my bloodlines.

Awaken me, God, as you fill me with your precious Holy Spirit, the same Holy Spirit that dwelled with Jesus, filled Him, and resurrected Him from the dead. Uncover every deception in me! Open my spiritual life to You and write my name in Your Lamb's Book of Life! I want You to overtake me and make us one as You and the Father are One. Thank You for restoring me and taking me from eternal darkness into Your eternal kingdom, where I dwell with You now and forever. I want to unite my desires with Yours, my spirit with Yours, my soul with Yours, and my body with Yours. For now and as long as I continue to abide in You, it will be in You that I live and move and have my being!

Note: If you have prayed this prayer for the first time or if it is your first time praying with understanding, please contact jesustodayministries.org as we would welcome the chance to celebrate with you as all of heaven! This prayer is your new beginning, but the walk through life is to be with God as our Head and us as His body. We need God, and we need each other, and we need to remain in the fellowship of the believers. Amen!

Prayer Points

Why does bad stuff happen to us? Psalm 91 declares God's protection of us. What we don't understand is how much more He protects us from what we do not see. Thank God for His mercy. Ask the Holy Spirit to take you deeper into how sin operates.

Doctors said I would remain disabled and in pain. What words have you believed? Bring them to God and seek what He spoke over you.

How serious are you taking your relationship with God or is Bible reading, praying, and fellowship simply a suggestion? We love God, but He always has more for us.

Do you expect God to do things your way?

Chapter 4: Union

Chapter 4: Union

As a child raised Catholic, I went to church every day. It meant the world to me, and I always felt this was a great honor for as long as I can remember. I never cared about the statues or the surrounding decorations. All I wanted was to kneel and talk to God because I knew He was there waiting for me. My prayers were simple but sincere: I would tell Him how thankful I was that He was real and truly loved me, and I always told Him everything that was going on in my life. As a child, I thought it was normal to talk to God all the time. I did not understand Catholic Latin, but the Word was read in English. I was so in love with God's Word it was as if He was talking to me.

As I got older, the sisters asked me to read the Word from the altar, and it was my privilege. I was learning more about Jesus, and the more I learned, the more I yearned. It wasn't until I became older that I understood the more time I spent in His presence, the more He released His grace to know Him deeper.

I started teaching children about the Bible at age fourteen, and this is now my fiftieth year. "Train up a child in the way he should go, and when he is old he will not depart from it" (Proverbs 22:6). My relationship with Him was a continuing walk to mature, as He did on the earth. I would talk to God about everything all the time, even if I was peeling potatoes for dinner. My close walk with Him was why I sought to understand why God did not prevent this accident.

Upon impact, the bottom of the steering wheel pushed into my stomach with such force that my major organs were deeply traumatized. The initial trauma from the accident was significant enough, but these issues became much worse as the years went by. Surgeons had to cut my belly open many times! Adhesions were taking over my insides. They are like strings of clear very tough bands that form as the body attempts to put itself back together after a serious injury, surgeries, or trauma. They cannot be seen through MRI and CT Scans, so as the pain worsened, doctors had to go through my bellybutton with a scope to see where the adhesions were. Eventually, the adhesions prevented free movement of the scope, so when I experienced severe pain—which had basically become my norm—the specialist would perform surgery again. The more they had to explore and or operate, the more adhesions formed. I had a few belly surgeries before the accident, but adhesions were never a concern. However, now I was in trouble because the trauma in my lower belly and the trauma from the seatbelt were out of control. The adhesions had wrapped around my organs, even as high as my gallbladder. The specialists were trying to keep me functioning by performing the surgeries to burn and cut these bands.

Although the doctors worked very hard, the truth was I was not feeling better, and I still was not functioning. My abdominal area had the most surgeries, but nothing with my belly could compare to the pain in my lower back. It felt like I was sitting on a butcher's knife! Despite that pain, I didn't allow doctors to touch my back, as I couldn't allow the adhesions to extend to my back. I was in agony! I remember reading the book of Job for moral support, asking the Holy Spirit to help me.

Job is a story of someone who trusted God while his possessions, children, and health were all stripped from him in one day. Throughout forty chapters, the Bible tells us that Job vocalized his feelings to God to deal with his pain. I could only mumble to God because my jaw would barely open. Again, all I could do was pray inwardly. I was so grieved from this accident that it literally was like a death. I could hear the quiet thought of the enemy telling me that God had forsaken me. I knew that could never happen, but I missed my time with God that this accident had stolen from me. I spent my first few years denying the doctors reports that I would remain like this, and now I was finding myself "bargaining with God." I would say, "God, if You fix this, I will do that." The Holy Spirit was teaching and training me to find my hope only in God, but as my hope spilled out, the bargaining led me in circles to ask, "Why, God, why?"

I was pounding on heaven's doors, asking and seeking God, but everything seemed to come back to me. I was comforted by Job because he spoke about what will happen to those who do not revere God, and I truly thought God and I were in "one accord." Just like me, Job questioned God about his condition. Then I saw this verse:

> For You write bitter things against me [in Your bill of indictment] and make me inherit and be accountable now for the iniquities of my youth (Job 13:26 AMPC).

I gasped, thinking I had finally found my answer. "Did this accident happen because of seeds I had sown in my past?" I cried out to God in my guilt for all I could think of. I knew I was forgiven, but I knew seedtime and harvest remained forever—and I could not bear to live like this for the rest of my life. I had drifted from God. My relationship with Him had become stagnant and was not growing. I looked and saw myself as a girl who hid in the Bible to be moral and religious. However, I was living in self-control and survival mode, which was my shield and protection against everything coming my way; but these methods did not work.

Without doubt I knew that God already paid the price for my healing and I was going to ask, seek, and knock until I was healed. I didn't want to just be a Christian; I wanted to be with Him! I continued in prayer to the best of my ability, and as the surgeries and years continued, I received some relief in some areas. My muscles were beginning to restore, but my soul and body felt like a tree whose roots were being ripped out. My nerves were regenerating through the holes of the muscles and misfiring like an electric shock! It felt like something was crawling within me.

One day during horrific spasms, the Lord explained to me how my spasming was a perfect illustration of what the body of Christ looks like when we are not in one accord with the Head—Jesus! When we are doing our own thing outside of God's truth, the world sees the church as having muscle spasms: a "leg" jumping one way and an "arm" going another. I was able to picture the disconnection of "Head" and "body" so clear because I physically experienced it every day. Oh, how I prayed for the body of Christ to come in one accord! The body was supposed to be in sync with each other as the Father, Son, and Holy Spirit. The horrific spasms reminded me to pray about the church every day.

Job was not the only one who lost everything in a day. One day David and his men came home to Ziklag from battling other nations, just to find out that the whole town had burned to the ground and that their wives and children were taken captive (1 Samuel 30:1-31). When you are in agony, each story in the Bible comes to life because you can truly feel and understand the suffering of others. So David and his mighty warriors cried until there were no tears left, and believe me, this is a very dry place! I began to put my feet in David's sandals. The Word said there were no bodies, so their wives and children were alive but taken as prisoners. I also felt that I had been taken prisoner in my own body. All throughout the stories of David, we know that his men were loyal and they would die for him, but this was the only time that the Word said they were ready to stone David. Oh, how I could relate to these men! They felt bitter, distressed, and grieved. So David asked Abiathar to bring him the ephod, and he inquired of the Lord. This was how David handled his situation and what I needed to see. He did not look to man but to God. David almost always turned inward to God. Job, on the other hand, focused on his troubles like I was. I was talking with God like Job but needed to look inward like David.

I trusted God's Word for my eternal promises, but did I trust God for my daily life?

The Holy Spirit kept guiding me through the words, "But David encouraged and strengthened himself in the Lord his God" (1 Samuel 30:6 AMPC). My flesh wondered how I could encourage myself. And then I started asking myself what seeds I could sow right now that would harvest in my health and my entire future. Job, David, and Pegge were so spiritually, emotionally, and physically distressed—and something within me "awakened." The pressure on the outside left me with nowhere to run except to dwell on the inside. No one could encourage me; I honestly didn't know what anyone could do. I could listen to people like Job, and I could see the anger and grief around my situation, but nothing in the world could change any of it. Job spoke what he believed, and David carefully watched his mouth. The Holy Spirit led me to replant my garden with God's seed.

This "seed" was released into me with knowledge from heaven. This knowledge was a weapon, and the seed was "praise." There were many days when I could only read one sentence from the Bible, and I would try so hard to meditate on it. I hung out in Psalms and Proverbs for many years. **Praise awakened my soul!** Whenever the thought came that all was lost, I encouraged myself with the words of David asking, "God, what would You have me do?" My praise for God was already within me. It was a well with deep, clean, and pure waters. Praise also made the demons flee! God's Word is the absolute instruction for anything I could ever face in my life, and the Bible is God's testimony of all He did to save me. I am His testimony! I would praise God for His promises to me even though I couldn't remember them line and verse. God inhabits the praises of His people. I knew the surest way to bring God close to me was by praising Him from the inside where, in my spirit, I could see my hands raise and my mouth open and where I could dance and run in His presence.

Did I truly trust God with my life, or was this just a bunch of words far from my heart? I had to trust that even though I hadn't received a warning from God about the impending accident, it was no surprise to Him. I came to accept that the accident happened and that God would bring forth my amazing testimony of how He brought me through it. What blocked this absolute trust was fear within me that held a place of authority. I was going to watch what God would do about all of this. I know God is Almighty Who knows and sees everything. Looking from His perspective, I could see the giant of fear next to the idol of self, feeding off each other in the depths of me. I felt like a hypocrite. I had so much pain, hurt, wounds, and offense stuffed inside of me. I was looking for God's accountability of why this incident happened and, through His love, found it was me who was unaccountable! I was like a "whitewashed tomb" that was not very clean on the inside. I trusted God's Word for my eternal promises, but did I trust God for my daily life? I wanted God to have all of me, but I wasn't even in line to offer this as my holy and living sacrifice.

I began to think of worst-case scenarios to test my faith to see, "Could I even trust God if this happened?" My faith was growing not in myself or the words written on the pages but in God—the Person. Would I fail to believe if my healing wasn't complete? While waiting, God just wanted me to come deeper into my knowledge of Him.

God wanted to use this time to mature me in sanctification. As my Teacher, the Holy Spirit led me in the everyday process of freely giving all my concerns to Him, separating me unto holiness. This is what I did as a child, but my childlike faith was snared with life and my way of doing it. The Holy Spirit wanted my soul, my mind, will, and emotions in one accord with my spirit and flesh. This is only done daily with God and me together. Now I understood the word *transformation*, and it was the same for Jesus when He walked on the earth. The transformation was dealing with how things appeared to my flesh as the enemy interfered with my spiritual life through my thoughts. God and I alone are to be involved with every aspect of my life! This brought such freedom from the screaming of my soul and body, pressuring me for the answers. When I wasn't taking my spiritual relationship seriously, I couldn't surrender, and therefore, I had no solution.

I had drifted! Things were good, and I was working ten to twelve hours a day on the farm. I loved it, and I loved my Lord. God was with me, but I was drifting in my personal God time, so everything remained stuffed in me, expecting me to figure it all out. This is, in my opinion, the greatest weapon the enemy has against us. He will get us involved with other things just enough for us drift from the Word and our time with our Creator. My King, in His goodness, was allowing me to see where I had let the enemy gain ground on me, and now that I wasn't functioning, he was coming for my faith and life. Whenever we sense hindrance, we can know the enemy is close at hand.

I had made an effort to quote Scripture to the enemy's onslaught to the best of my ability, but now I depended on the Holy Spirit to bring me a Word as I fought through the pain and the painkillers. How I longed to have memorized Scripture! But even if I had, my mind was so injured that I struggled to finish a thought, leaving me dependent on God. In reality, I was helpless, but in this stage of my life, I was trained for war! Who would've thought? But praise God that He sees us differently than we see ourselves. Although I wanted to lift my hands in praise physically, I only could spiritually. Then the Holy Spirit enlightened me with another valuable weapon of heaven. I would never have imagined "being still" as a weapon of power, but it truly is! I learned that when I became "still," only God was in control. When I was "still," it was as if I was hidden under the "impenetrable" shield of God. I was under

His protection, and the enemy's weapons would bounce off of me.

The Holy Spirit began pinging every time the enemy attempted to put me down or make me believe lies. When I was struggling before, these weapons would hurt me. I could watch the enemy's words like bullets, reminding me of what the doctors said or the fiery darts of the enemy that would hit my flesh and torment my soul. However, this time it was different: under God's shield was a position of maturing to life in the spirit realm where I would be still and watch. I was like a "watchwoman on the wall." As I became still, things started to change.

Even my secret place was a "war zone." I could hear the pounding of pain, which sounded like "drums of war." The Holy Spirit in me was absolutely alive, and as the Spirit brought to my remembrance the battles of those before me, I thought of Peter. Jesus told Peter that the enemy wanted to sift him like wheat from the chaff. I saw myself as that piece of grain being vigorously shaken to the core to separate me from all that covered me. The enemy wanted to shake Peter's faith in hopes that he would fall away (Luke 22:31-34). Remember how Peter told Jesus he would die with him? Well, the enemy knows a few things about the power of fear that Peter and I did not. Peter was wounded by his own disloyalty, and I also felt deeply disloyal. Loyalty was extremely important to me, and the enemy knew it. Peter's failure encouraged me because I knew that it wasn't the end of his story; instead, it became a stepping stone to come closer into the kingdom of heaven.

In reality, I was helpless, but in this stage of my life, I was trained for war! Who would've thought?

In my case, I felt like a failure, and the enemy wanted to use this weapon against me. He bombarded me with thoughts like, *How could someone in my condition fulfill God's call on my life?* The enemy knew that I feared not being able to continue living life as I knew it. The enemy wanted me to believe that God did this to me, that I would not be healed and that this was God's intention for my life. I would remain disabled with a great prayer life. That was my snare, but the light of the Word taught me a valuable lesson through Peter's failure: what matters at this stage of my life is how I will respond! How would I react when the devil tried to sift my faith and make me feel useless and worthless? He was after my strength, and this made me realize that I have some left. I had the strength of God! I had to remind myself that God doesn't make junk. We are the treasuries of heaven here on the earth. I could feel the joy of God filling within me! The joy of the Lord is my strength, and whenever I needed more of God's strength, I simply had to praise Him!

The Lord was also showing me how the enemy manipulates people with his thoughts and his symptoms. The Holy Spirit was exposing how I swallowed the enemy's lies in my soul, and the symptoms would show up in my body, and then I would speak them into existence through my mouth and actions. This was how I had been seeding my garden. I was saved, yet trapped in my lack of knowledge in the enemy's strongholds. I did not want to live as an enemy spy who occasionally visited the kingdom of light! This was preventing Jesus from freely ministering to me, and this is why I would only let Him in so far. The enemy had taken far too much ground, and I knew I was agreeing with him with my victim mindset. Honestly, I think there were days when I was more in union with the enemy's emotions than with God. Why was I allowing it? I quickly could see that if I am not real with God and myself, then the enemy will load me with his fake, counterfeit ways of operating, striving to be like him instead of being in Christ!

God, why won't You heal me?

God is a Spirit, I am a spirit, and the enemy is a spirit. Everything takes place in the spirit realm, and what we see on the outside is the fruit thereof. The only way I could release myself from all of this was by never again accepting partial victory. I was not quitting. Jesus did not quit, and He rose healed from that tomb. My fear was no longer about if or when God would heal me, nor was it about what I did wrong. My fear is of my Commander in Chief and His overcoming power against the enemy. Victory belongs in my hands! My Lord was fighting for me, and my entire being belonged to Him. God wanted me to drive out the inhabitants of the land who do not line up with His Word. The Holy Spirit would destroy every foundation where I lacked truth, and the enemy's strongholds were coming down. I only wanted God to remain and to dwell with Him. I knew if I didn't drive out the enemy, just like the story of the Israelites, the adversaries would remain as pricks in my eyes and thorns in my side, and they would vex me. God wanted me to see what was in my heart, and this humbled me. My life would never be the same!

My healing was my weakest point. The devil knew it and was testing me through the pain of my body and soul. Sometimes I would win a battle, and sometimes I continued screaming at the devil, yelling at myself, crying, and asking, "Lord, why won't You heal me?" His response was so calm, "I already have!" Then I would ask Him, "Where is the physical evidence of my healing"? What a patient and long-suffering Father He is! He was comforting, caring, and speaking His love over me day and night. The Holy Spirit led me to the verse in the Bible that says to lay hands on the sick, and they will recover. So I would lay hands on myself where I could reach without much progress, but my faith was growing!

I remember one day very well because my middle back was aching, and the pain meds did nothing; I had the choice to either scream in pain or do something! So I thought to lay my hands on my back, but this only would work if I had that mobility. I was so desperate that I laid my hands on the edge of my bedroom door and said, "I am sending the Word of God into you, door." I said that with all the faith that I had! Then I leaned up against the door and physically felt God's peace entering my spine. I could feel pressure leaving the area! I had never heard or seen anyone do something like this before. I was being transformed by the pounding of the pain with a desire to pound back at the enemy!

Prayer:

Dad, I ask You to bring understanding to us that we are Your family. We are not scattered, defenseless sheep without a Shepherd, as this is how the enemy steals from us. Thank You for showing me that there is no sin or ugliness that I cannot bring to You for healing and deliverance. Father, help me remember that if my actions are not reflecting Your love, it is not You. Teach me, Lord, to bring myself daily before You as a living sacrifice to unload all this stuff instead of stuffing it within me. Holy Spirit, please make me sensitive to every thought, word, deed, and action that does not line up with the Word of God, so I can catch and rebuke it according to Your Word before the seed enters me.

You and the kingdom of heaven are my life's focus. Holy Spirit, please teach me to be one with You as You are with Jesus, so our kingdom authority is a united front against the enemy. I am hungry to receive more of Your training in kingdom knowledge, wisdom, understanding, discernment, and revelation, as my identity in You is being restored. Holy Spirit, I ask You to reveal every plan, strategy, and influence of how the enemy operates against Your body. I want to defend the gates of Your church and my temple with the fear of You. I want to take back everything the enemy has stolen from us! I no longer fear the devil or my own way of doing things.

Union

Thank You, Jesus, my great Intercessor, that You continue to pray for me day and night. Thank You forever for saving me and all of humanity. We are so blessed! I want everyone to have their spiritual blinders removed, so in You, we are undefeatable NOW! Thank You for never giving up on me. I am not quitting. All the time I was waiting, You were waiting on me to rise into my identity in Your family!

Prayer Points

Union comes when we understand how our spirit is to depend on the Holy Spirit within us for all things. If our soul - (mind, will, emotions and our character traits) does what it wants then recognize that it is "self" that is in control. We must submit our souls —our thoughts, ways and deeds to our spiritual life.

Union brings understanding of why we must pray, praise, read and take time for a relationship with our God. This is what Jesus did. When we do not we are "drifting."

Write out your God schedule (time with God) and let life abide around it.

Start a new prayer habit by asking the Holy Spirit, "What do You want me to do?" Be still and surrender all those thoughts and worries to Him.

Praise God and be filled with His healing light. When we praise God we are not thinking about ourselves or our problems. Receive the King!

What idol is reigning in you? Once you can see it you can give it to God for destruction before it steals more from you.

Chapter 5:
I Surrender

Chapter 5: I Surrender

For five years, the only thing I saw changing was me losing more and more, so I decided to make a deal with my body. The doctors said I would remain this way for the rest of my life, and when my mind looked outside of my spirit life, I believed what I saw. I was becoming stagnant with no activity. I was waiting on God to heal me and knew He was also waiting on me. **Was God waiting for me to get up and get over myself?**

One day I spoke to my body, saying, "You won't stop hurting me, and now *I* am going to hurt you, and then we both have agreed!" You keep me in pain, so in pain, I am going back to work. God didn't want me to harm myself, and I'm sure the devil probably enjoyed me doing his job for him, but I made a decision to help God by standing in faith. While my healing was not yet manifested, I made a plan to regain my life. I will never forget thinking that me helping God was a good thing. I wanted to start doing some sort of exercise and talked myself into believing that this would make me feel better and bring hope to my senses.

How can anyone go wrong with some exercise? I was still having surgeries and promised my doctors that I would "behave myself," but I lied! I had no intention of letting this accident have any more power over me. I came to a place where I was done with this whole mess. I had a farm to run! I told my mind I was changing the word *disabled* to *enabled*. In my rebellion, I used the Word of God as my legal document. How about that? I was going to call what was not as though it was! I was getting no exercise at all, so why wouldn't my body be hurting? My mind was playing tricks on me!

My reasoning for doing all of this was because I could not stop fighting for my freedom, but my motive was pride and self-will. I told myself that I was not giving up on the promises of God, so, like Abraham's wife Sarah, I decided to give Him some help (Genesis 16:1-6). I got on the mower and bounced in the yard, cutting the grass. Oh, the sheer agony of pain! But I figured that I would suffer anyway and managed to get a small bit of the lawn done. Actually, one of my helpers looked out the barn window and saw me and came out screaming! He helped me off the mower as if I was a hundred-year-old woman having a temper tantrum, and to be honest, I was stuck in that position. It took two helpers to lift me off of the mower. What was I thinking? This was the war I lived with every day in my soul.

Living with adhesions was a full-time job. How full should I stuff myself? I would wonder. Should I fast to try and break them before they strangled my intestines, which could kill me? The meds would constipate me, and the laxatives would empty me! My stomach wall was literally splitting apart. If I did nothing, I could form a hernia. If I did something, I could form a hernia. Either way, the doctors would do more surgery to sew me back together, which would create more adhesions. What can you do when your body has such control over you? If you are not familiar with what a hernia is, it's when a person's organs, intestines, or tissues protrude through the split of the muscular wall of the stomach, and yes, it is extremely painful!

I remember one surgery where the doctors had to repair eight hernias in my belly at one time. After I woke up from anesthesia, my surgeon threatened me: *"If I see you on this table again, I will put iron mesh in your belly."* I just said "okay," but to be honest, I did not want to see him again either. What did he think I was doing? Trick riding on my horses? My soul was so traumatized. My attitudes, my intellect, and every chamber of my being were in a war. Imagining the pain of just the hernias would be more than enough for most people to handle, but this high pain level had now become almost "normal" to me. With all the splitting and the binding of the adhesions, nothing could compare to the pain in my lower back. There was no tolerance, position, or drug to relieve this pain.

After being discharged from the hospital, one of my employees brought me back to the farm. It was late afternoon, and the rest of my employees had already gone home for the day. I was lying on the couch, wondering how all of my animals were. My workers kept telling me that everything was okay, but I had to see it for myself. There was no one there to update me, and I had been gone for three days. I was so used to being in control! My mind was thinking about my animals, and before I knew it, my soul convinced my flesh that I really needed to go see them. They were my responsibility! For the record, I had 180,000 chickens plus rabbits, sheep, goats, pigs, horses, and cows—not to mention fields that needed tending. I was not planning to work or lift anything; I just wanted to lay my eyes upon my animals. I had promised myself to do just one walk per day to encourage my healing progress. In my mind, I came up with every excuse under the sun to convince myself that this walk was necessary.

I knew my mind had the power to either bring me closer to the light or the darkness.

Deep inside, I knew I was wrong but still did it with God's help, and by that, I mean I knew He was watching me as I hobbled to the barn. Oh, the craftiness of my soul! When it was almost dark out, I began walking just four hundred feet to the first barn. Oh, how much I missed moving! I felt I had overcome and won a great victory but totally forgot that I would have to climb three stairs to enter the building. To be honest, I could have called my neighbor to come and check everything for me, but my motive wasn't about the animals. I went because I was rebelling! My goal was to regain just a small glimpse of control. I was lying to God and myself. My mind told my body that it was created to move and that the "Boss" was back! This time my body was not the problem, my mind was a battlefield, and I believed I found a strategy to win! How long had my vain thoughts remained in expectation of resurrecting my past?

As a farmer, it was customary for me to wake up every morning at 3 a.m. so I had time to pray on my knees and exercise before starting chores in the daylight. Since the accident, I continued waking up at 3 a.m., although now it was a reminder of all I could not do but was fighting to regain. Even as I could barely sleep through the night, 3 a.m. became my customary time in prayer with the Lord. I would tell Him everything and ask Him to help me. I would pout, doubt, whine, beg, stipulate, negotiate, cry, laugh, forget what I said—and start all over again. I would scream to release the anguish of self, and still, I could feel His presence so strongly—even in my rebellion—and I honestly wondered why He did not turn from me. I could see how much my mind was in trouble, and I didn't want to become seared and hard against God.

I watched how my mind was trying to grab control of my spiritual life. It was enough to stop my healing, and I could not let this happen. I knew my mind had the power to either bring me closer to the light or the darkness. When you are in a place where you don't even want to talk about the situation you see is not changing, but instead worsens, you feel alone—even in His presence. In those moments, I would picture my beautiful Savior alone hanging on that cross, looking up to heaven and asking His Father the question. His was "why," and mine was "when." I never thought anyone could find such comfort gazing upon the blood-torn flesh of my Jesus. Before the accident, I didn't even like to read about the crucifixion, but now it was my place of comfort! He understood where I was at and what I was going through, and I would again find rest in Him and fall asleep. Jesus was with me.

I would pray in tongues, journal, minister to God, and ask Him tons of questions. When I say that I would minister to God, it would be simply spending time with Him. I longed to get my mind off myself, so I would dwell on Him. My time with Him became focused on Him—not just what I wanted from Him. I watched how much He cared about me and for me! I had nothing to offer Him but myself, and I was what He longed for! I started caring about Him, His desires, and His needs, and this taught me to care about myself. I know when I pray that He was moving on my behalf. He just wanted me to be there with Him. When I wasn't in "spirit mode," I was miserable! God was listening to both sides of me. He knew the "real" me: my mind, attitudes, character, sin, nature, every emotion, and every wicked and evil thing that could come from them. I could not hide in His presence, and as He uncovered my deepest issues, He patiently taught me to submit them to Him and stop squirming and wrestling against Him.

Through the loss of control, I found the battle I was losing was more than physical

Through the continued hospital stays, surgeries, and rehabilitation, I learned to remain both naked and vulnerable before Him. I could not let my circumstances have control! I felt stuck in the same circle as the Israelites, wandering around the same mountain in the desert while they learned to abandon their past, discover their true identity, and remember all that my Savior has done. What's interesting is the more Jesus healed me, the more other parts of me were falling apart. It reminded me so much of the Israelites! God was so close to them that even their clothes and shoes never wore out, but they were a mess—whining over leeks and onions (Numbers 11:5). I no longer asked, "Why did God?" I now asked, "Why was I behaving the way I did, believing and settling in my striving, controlling and planning as if this was my true identity?" I wanted to learn from them, so I had to surrender fully. Through daily surrender came a union and agreement with God. Through this submission, I was able to see what God saw when He looked at my heart—my whole being!

My spirit loved God and I was abiding with Him, but it wasn't enough; God also wanted my whole heart, soul, mind, and strength. I had to learn who I was as a human being. My heart is the source of how I feel, think, act, love, my intentions, and how I discern right from wrong. My soul is my mind, will, emotions, and everything about me as a person. My mind was created to work with God, but it also has its own opinions and can make decisions apart from Him. My mind leads my soul and must be renewed daily through the Word of God. My physical body connects me through my senses to express what is going on within me. I knew that my physical body would be restored, but my strength was not to serve myself but the Lord. I had not yet grasped how intricately I was created.

The Lord began showing me how the battle has always been about much more than just our flesh. It has been like that since the beginning. Satan aimed at the mind of Eve in the garden, coming against her soul's emotions and intellect with the pleasant view of the fruit, her mind's feelings to eat of it, and her heart's desire not to disobey the Lord. The same tactic was used on me, to hit my flesh and cause injury, and hit my soul to drift my heart from the truth and infect my eternal relationship with God. Through the loss of control of my body, I found that my soul was losing a battle, and it was more than just physical healing; God wanted me to surrender my whole heart, soul, mind, and strength to Him so He could keep me whole! God was always to be first in my life, but in reality, I hadn't surrendered—and this was stopping my transformation process into the likeness of Jesus—the resurrected Jesus!

The world would say that my faith was "foolish," so I strived to prove to all, including myself, that I would be healed. First, I had to learn to "be" in God and let Him live through me and with me, just like Adam and Eve were with Him before the fall of man. This sounded great and was something I thought I was already doing, but nothing was scarier than seeing the craftiness of my own being! My spirit was willing to pray and obey, but my mind and emotions would agree with my flesh. This was war!

I didn't want to agree with the devil and the world by allowing my sensual, carnal, and worldly mind to be controlled by my own passions –boastful and arrogant, gratifying unholy desires, to make me destitute of my higher spiritual life. This is what would happen if I would not surrender everything to God! A debased mind is ruled by the demonic and not God. "All the ways of a man are pure in his own eyes, but the Lord weighs the spirits" (Proverbs 16:2 NKJV).

As I mentioned earlier, the weapons of my warfare were not physical, but they are mighty before God for the overthrow and destruction of strongholds of arguing, reasonings, theories, and every proud and lofty thing that sets itself up against the truth of God. Second, along with God, I had to discern every thought and purpose by taking them captive into the obedience of Christ, or my soul would hold me as a prisoner. What if God never had this opportunity to stir up my unsullied mind by way of remembrance? My heavenly Father wanted me to be mindful of Him, that even though so much of me was already transformed into His likeness, it would be wrong to think there isn't more junk in me. This was to be a daily walk of giving myself to Him. God had cracked through my "eggshell," uncovering my inner being. This is where I was shown the way to give my mind and very essence to Him.

Just like Moses, who had to leave the camp and get away from everyone to go to the tent of meeting and fall on his face before God, I had to do the same. The fullness of God was blocked by the mishandling of my soul and how it interacted with my mind and my flesh. Adam and Eve failed in this—and they knew and walked with God in person! These sins were holding back many good things that God provided for me. God gave me time to understand and repent with Him. He wanted me to awaken to the understanding of being chastised to surrender so that I could be delivered from destruction. The strength to do this is found in God. The Scripture says, "casting down arguments and every high thing that exalts itself against the knowledge of God, bringing every thought into captivity to the obedience of Christ, and being ready to punish all disobedience when your obedience is fulfilled" (2 Corinthians 10:5-6). I had to learn from the Word how to chastise my being through His discernment to stay free.

My soul now understood its purpose to watch daily and deny the pull of my mind, the world, what I saw and heard, and even what I could touch with my hands—like a doctor's report—and bring everything into the truth of the Word of God. I needed His Word to wrap around me as tight as the adhesions that covered my inner organs. These spiritual boundaries changed everything! With God I would now chastise my enemies. These were spiritual boundaries that I was not paying attention to before. I could envision the battlefield within my being by discerning myself, and this was how God showed me He looks upon the heart of man. I am so much more than a spirit, soul, and body. I am a soldier in the army of God with boundaries to protect. I have to keep the pollution out of my temple. I didn't ever want my mind cooperating as an enemy of God again. And yet, this task seemed so much bigger than me. I surrendered all to God to teach me self-control. I didn't know how He will do this, but I knew He taught the ocean to control its boundaries, so this shouldn't be a problem for Him.

The Holy Spirit reminded me of Joseph's story (Genesis 37-50). He had such a good future and great dreams, and everything turned out wonderfully for him in the end. But

I was more focused on how Joseph dealt with his thoughts and wondered how much the enemy and his surroundings tormented him. He was kidnapped and sold to slave traders by his brothers. Joseph even married a foreign woman, yet God was with him. He was in a foreign land with foreign gods, the very thing his being was trained not to do. I was in a bed surrounded by everything I never thought could happen to a believer. I couldn't read much of the Word physically, but God was doing everything through the surrender of my heart, soul, mind, and strength. I am sure Joseph had to continually stir his mind up in remembrance of God because even in the filth of prison, he was a bright light. God brought success to everything Joseph touched, and Father kept him faithful!

Even in the darkest times of Joseph's life he was blessed with finances, management, and farming, yet everyone around him was an unbeliever. He even bragged on God way before he met Pharaoh. The relentless pressure Joseph faced brought him deep within himself, and as he was going through it all, the Egyptians knew of Joseph's God. He came into a very high calling, but it was his surrender to God that brought Joseph into a place of rest from his external struggle. Joseph was second in power after Pharaoh; God showed me that even the most gifted of His people could lose the battle in their hearts, soul, mind, and strength if they are not surrendered to God. In my brokenness, I was still blessed and preached about my love for my Savior, even in my mess. I would still catch a ride to church in between surgeries to teach kids in Sunday school. I can't imagine what they thought about me telling them about having victory in Jesus as they watched my struggle walking and moving but trusting God to finish the rest.

My recovery was to begin on the inside and not from my flesh.

As we learn to use His words to destroy the enemies of our souls, God gives us very powerful weapons: "'Is not My word like a fire?' says the Lord, 'and like a hammer that breaks the rock in pieces'" (Jeremiah 23:29 NKJV). My soul is the door of my heart, and I am to keep my heart with all diligence unto the Lord. My heart is to be guarded, for out of it flows the issues of life. I needed more than just healing for my body; I needed healing of my very being. The Word tells me the thoughts of God, and this is what I am to think, and any foreign god needs to be destroyed. I needed to clear the land just like the Israelites, and their strategies given by God were all making perfect sense to me. Every enemy they were told to cast out was an enemy to their soul!

In my suffering, I found my spiritual knees on which I would exercise through warfare by using the weapons of heaven. My new job was to be a soldier and a gatekeeper of my temple. I didn't want to be spiritually dead while walking around telling everyone how much I love God without having an understanding of the stubborn rebellion in my very being. I knew that there was only one suffering allowed after the atonement of Jesus Christ, which was persecution. If I was beaten or chained or spit on or slapped because of my loyalty to Jesus Christ, that was acceptable, and I would be rewarded in heaven, but being broken and defeated after the atonement was absolutely "illegal." I had surrendered to the wrong side, and I repented. I allowed the enemy, my being, and the world to trespass against me! God was so proud to help me up and dust me off! I was being transformed by the renewing of my mind, and my job was to remain in the Word of God and dwell in His presence while ruling this temple.

I saw the truth from the Truth! It was never about what kind of a family I was born into, where I went to church, or what kind of school I attended. It was never about how much money I made, what I did, or how many friends I had. It was never about my cars or the size of my house. It was never about who I was married to or divorced from. It was never about if my children obeyed me or messed up. It was never about if my pastor was in diligent prayer for me or my doctor understood me. It was never about politics or who was president. It was never about what nation I was born into or what culture I was raised in. It wasn't about wars or rumors of wars. It was never about pandemics or financial crashes. It was never about whether I would become famous or remain a praying woman on my bed. It wasn't about if I was a slave or I ran the country, as these are all just distractions to take my focus off the wellbeing of my eternal life that began the day I was saved.

These are all distractions like vanity to ever so carefully and quietly drift me away from the Truth. If the enemy could pull my mind, my soul would follow from the path of the Shepherd, and I would not see that I had drifted! Inside of me is the kingdom of heaven. With the ability to surrender all to God daily, I had found my true wealth! My recovery was to begin on the inside and not from my flesh. Now I knew how to take what was already inside me and bring it from the kingdom into the earth. All of God's words and promises were sitting right inside of me. I am a spirit from heaven that carries God Himself on this earth surrounded by stuff, and from this position of living in the realm of the spirit, God wanted to finish what He had started.

I had been trying to "work the Word" in my favor, but now the kingdom of heaven was alive and working from within me. Cain did not surrender and brought God his external offering, while Abel was blessed by God through a life of internal sacrifice and surrender in relationship to God. I was now able to see that when I was healthy, had total control of my life, and believed that all was well, in reality, I was more naked, poor, and blind than in my brokenness now. How arrogant I was to think of God the way I did! Unless I continued to surrender my being to the Holy Spirit, I could not see the sinful roots established in me. Until I continue to submit my being to the Holy Spirit, I could not see all of His gifts within me!

Prayer:

Lord, You are God! There truly is none like You. You showed me the inner me and revealed how intricately You made me. You showed me how fullness in You is attained through my surrender. You showed me how to remove the blocks that kept us from flowing as one. I used to feel alone, even while I was in Your presence, but now I know how to find You every day! I was broken, miserable, controlling, mean, bossy, believed in myself, and thought I was reflecting You. You are love, joy, peace, patience, goodness, kindness, faithfulness, gentleness, and self-control.

Show me how to relate to You as You deserve! Teach me how to treat myself the way You treat me! Bring that gulf between heaven and earth ever closer as You teach me who we are together! I am sorry for trying to recreate You into my image! You are not like the world or the enemy. You don't bring the pain. You bring the recovery! Thank You for allowing me to repent and see where I am being pulled from You. Thank You, my Good Shepherd, for teaching me how to chastise my enemies. You are a Good Father, and no one could ever love me like You!

Prayer Points

The accident had been controlling my life, but I wanted control over everything. What is taking control over your life? Are you able to submit it to God?

Control lays heavy weights upon us because we are not lifting it to the Lord.

Where is your flesh controlling you?

Where is your soul controlling you? Are these godly thoughts?

Will you trust God with your daily life?

Chapter 6: Gifts

Chapter 6: Gifts

What was God's next move in the healing of my broken mess? My racing thoughts could not be allowed to steal the good memories of my life before the accident. I was desperate to remember and hold onto my dreams, my journal entries, and the prophetic words spoken over me. I could see and remember some of what I was taught in school and in church, and I was so grateful! How I blessed my parents for taking me to church every Sunday and being strict with me to teach me the narrow path. I used to wonder why I had to learn some of the things I did in school and at home, never realizing how it all comes together making sense in your future. I had plenty of time to lay still to think, and this is where God met me in the training of how to heal my mind and memory through His Word and His Blood.

I was dwelling in the soul of my crushed temple, warring daily to get my mind to stop fighting me. My memory was bruised, grieved, and crushed, and my emotional healing was to be found again at the cross and in the Word. Yet after dozens of procedures and surgeries and all of the gifted knowledge in the medical field, doctors did not and could not bring me to the point of healing. Years after the initial damage from the accident, my body was worn. New reports showed that my spine was deteriorating, and I was diagnosed with deteriorating disc disease. The medications were causing me to gain so much weight, which was also taking a toll on my spine and joints. I was also diagnosed with fibromyalgia. Fibromyalgia is widespread pain throughout the nerves and muscles of my body. I was angry because I was scared, but I was furious with these new reports. I told my doctor that Jesus healed all of my "diseases."

I had no problem holding God accountable to His Word that I am already healed, but was I being accountable to Him by pushing my body beyond what it could handle? I knew He didn't want me to give up the fight, I knew I was maturing in faith, but should I continue having surgeries? I believed God to heal me! I also knew that He created science and that there was a time and a place where doctors and surgeries and medication were needed, and I knew He was also healing me through all of this. I didn't know what my mind or body could handle anymore or how many more scars I could take! I was becoming depressed, but that was unacceptable, so I tried to focus on God.

Despite all the pain and embracing the cross, I kept envisioning my race. I was coming out of this tomb to finish the calling of my life (see Acts 20:24). I thanked God for the gift of His Holy Spirit; the same Spirit that brought

Jesus out of the tomb was living in me. I knew every problem of my life was in that tomb with Him, and He was out, totally healed from brokenness. I could not fathom how He carried all of our pain and sin, but His death was my "gift"—and I wasn't going to take His gift for granted.

I had no idea how many emotions I had and how they connected to survive.

People who witnessed my suffering said if they were in my shoes, they "would not even attempt to get out of the bed." I was tired of how misunderstood I was. It wasn't about what I looked like on the outside but who I was on the inside. I saw the disunity in humanity, and this taught me more about myself. Recovering from surgery while still struggling to read my Bible, I watched Christian television. I could watch ten different preachers teach on healing in one day, but nothing changed, and they did not bring answers. People of faith believed that I wasn't healed because I didn't have faith—but I did! Some of them blamed me saying, "If you had faith, you would stop taking that pain medicine!" I understood that when people do not have answers, we all blame something or someone besides ourselves because of the wounds of our souls.

The words we say to other people have such a profound effect. Sometimes we speak so carelessly, without thinking of what our words could do to the soul of that person. I condemned myself for the pills and stopped taking them, and that night I ended up in the emergency room, getting lectured by doctors to stop listening to people! I stopped taking the pills that day just to see if my miracle had occurred. Preachers on TV encouraged me to "fake it till I make it!" and you can only imagine how I looked as I faked healing! I had to keep my soul from becoming entangled with the thoughts and plans of others. This left me even more isolated, but in this place, I learned to judge my own ways of thinking and believing with God. I battled for my answers for everything. I knew Adam was created by God, and he messed up, but I was begotten by God, saved, and brought into the kingdom of heaven. I thought this meant that my healing should be quick. **What was I missing?**

These questions were a fire in my soul! There were days when I would wake up, and my mind would think it was time to get up, but my body wouldn't move. My mind said to go, but the only thing that moved was my eyelashes. I learned to thank God that I could blink my eyes. I prayed so hard for all the people who were homebound and not able to attend church. God showed me how many people are alone with no one to share His life, and I committed to remember and pray for them even after my healing. How many gifts had I taken for granted? Some days my body would move, then become stiff, then turn hard as a rock, and I would have to lie on my bed and wait. Many years had passed. My altar of sacrifice was my body, and from this rock, I cried out to God to deliver me! God gave me two spiritual seeds from heaven that became planted within me: hunger and faith! Hunger and faith, watered with my tears, were my fight to live, and with my fight came more confidence with God who was right there with me and could have healed me in a breath.

Meanwhile, my left shoulder was no longer able to move and just hung by my side. Six months before this surgery, I had to train myself to use only one hand. I was honestly shocked that my right shoulder was moving because my right trapezius and the muscles under it were very badly damaged, to the point that it still hurt to touch all these years later. I believed God to heal my shoulders supernaturally, but it didn't happen. The surgeon said that my shoulder was "frozen" and needed to be repaired. My whole being cried within me at the thought of another surgery. By now, I had gone through over twenty surgeries, and I stirred up my faith and found desperation. I acted like a tough soldier, telling my doctor how many painkillers I had at home, and off we went.

Oh, my Jesus! I was now home alone, and the morphine was wearing off. The pain was so bad that I thought I had reached the point where it was more than I could bear. I heard the devil taunt me again with this same Scripture saying, "I thought God would never give you more than you can handle." I cried, I screamed, and I yelled to God! "Help me, Father; this is getting beyond my human strength!" God pointed out to me where I had a few more potent painkillers left from previous surgeries. I thanked Him that I had been bit by a brown recluse spider eight months earlier because they gave me analgesic patches, and I had two left. With the two remaining powerhouse patches, I still took two Vicoden every two hours. Fear gripped me as I wondered if I had lost my pain tolerance.

My surgeon had me so bandaged up after surgery that not an inch of my shoulder could move until the muscles began to heal. I, of course, had no idea what took place during the surgery until the follow-up appointment one week later.

I told him about the pain, and he told me the surgery ended up being much more than a "repair." My entire muscle was ripped from my arm to my shoulder, to the point where the surgeon did not even have enough good muscle salvageable to put back on the bone. So the doctors decided to cut part of my scapula bone to be able to reattach the muscles. Unfortunately, this was not the only problem! The ball and socket of my shoulder were so messed up that the surgeon had to dislocate my shoulder to remove and shave the splintered pieces.

When the layers of bandages were removed on that follow-up appointment, I could see a black-and-blue of his entire arm, hand, and fingers across my chest. He told me the bruises were from the amount of pressure needed to re-attach my arm. He said he had to lean over me to push the arm back into the socket and then finish putting me back together. The surgery was so brutal my body was traumatized, aggravating everything, including the fibromyalgia causing every muscle in my body to become hard as a rock while my nerves kept misfiring. **How did Jesus take all of His pain?** The soldiers dislocated His shoulder for my sins and the sins of the world without anesthesia! I kept asking Jesus to unite my pain to His because I knew His pain was past tense, and I couldn't handle my present pain any longer.

It took months for me to lift that one shoulder. I couldn't sleep or fix my hair. I couldn't even hook my bra. I needed help to get dressed. I had reached a new low. I had to take my mind off the trauma, so I thanked God for everything in my life that was working! I was thanking Him that it was my left arm and not my right. I was more helpless than ever, and there were some very unhealthy emotions growing within me. I had no idea how many emotions I had and how they connected to survive. I knew I had to dump the anger before I went to sleep. **"Okay, God, what do you want me to do?"** I asked. He wanted me to read healing Scriptures out loud! That may sound easy, *but I couldn't even hold the Book, let alone open my mouth more than two fingers!*

Reading the Word and doing the Word are totally different.

After my tantrum with God, I knew only He would make it happen, even if I had to mumble the Word—and mumbling was now something I had become good at. I bought the digital Bible to listen to both on cassette tapes and then CDs. Through both of them, I was told to make recordings with my own voice of healing Scriptures, adding any prayer that I sensed God was giving. When I was back on the couch or bed, which was most of the time, I would push play and began listening to me speaking the Word out loud with my own voice. Believe it or not, this seriously made a change in my life, as I could feel the power of God through my words! God wanted me to learn how to use His Word and my mouth to wield the sword of the Spirit with power.

I was still having a terrible time trying to remember His Word and to even speak, but I cooperated with Him and had the recordings. Sometimes I would try to memorize one verse at a time, and even if I were successful that day, it would usually be gone by the next. I was trapped in my lack of knowledge. When you are hanging between life and death, the Bible is no longer just a book of rice paper and ink. Every word within becomes Jesus Christ Himself speaking, praying, and encouraging you as if you met face to face! Before, I didn't take His Word as seriously as life or death, and I didn't take the words I spoke seriously. What a very dangerous place to be! I began to understand the difference between speaking what my emotions and mind were thinking and feeling and stating what Jesus spoke or how He remained silent. I could talk with God about everything within, but the enemy was waiting to trap me with my spoken words.

I was now watching my temple to guard the words that came out of my mouth. I could think it and feel it, but I tried so hard not to speak it, and this took training. Reading the Word and doing the Word are totally different! The Holy Spirit wanted me to agree with Him in prayer. **The power of God is released through agreement in prayer!** No wonder my healing had not yet manifested as my words were not agreeing with God or representing what He accomplished or promised to me. I was snaring myself and keeping myself bound in pain. Of course, God knew all about this, but my journey with Him is all about awakening to who I am in Him. He wanted me to know how to defeat every enemy—including sickness. My faith level had to mature, so I surrendered my mouth and asked the Holy Spirit to be God through me! Was I healed yet? No; I was a work in progress.

Once we see the battle and notice how many people around us suffer, we won't be able to sit still—no, we will have to fight!

I was seriously infuriated by how much the enemy still gets away with, even after the shed Blood of Jesus Christ. Year after year, I could notice how the enemy used the same basic approach to annoy and spite me, to the point where I believed he had nothing new under the sun. The pain would sear through my nerves and my muscles, and I would scream, "God, I am in pain, BUT BY YOUR STRIPES, I AM HEALED! I shunned the devil to the best of my ability. God and I absolutely wanted the wicked cut off. And still, almost every day, I could not stop the doubt and insecurity from creeping into my belief.

Warfare was at an all-time high. God gave me His authority over everything, including the "creeps," and I needed more training about how to wield that sword of the Spirit. With a closed mouth, I yelled, "Devil, you messed up. You caused this accident to happen, and I am suffering, but I am alive in Christ. You've been talking smack to me and getting away with it, but the Holy Spirit is teaching me to cut off your wickedness from my soul with the Word of God. No wonder you want me to doubt. You are the father of lies, and now I know how you kill, steal, and destroy" (John 10:10).

I was no longer in fear of what he could do to me next. I was going to remind him to fear my God! The enemy was losing his control over me. I realized that the reason he was coming so hard against me was because I had not been conquered! Not only was God teaching me more about deliverance, but I was starting to enjoy myself. I told the devil that God was promoting me and that all this warfare and training would birth so many future miracles. Now I understood that every time he attacked me proved that God and I were winning! How could I ever believe all things were possible through Jesus' atonement if I wasn't in the battle? How do you know how to fight your enemy if you can't see or know how they operate?

We are warned not to be deceived, but deception is usually cloaked to blind us. It affects our heart, soul, mind, and strength, our families, and the generations after us, but an unseen enemy can gain much ground unless we are maturing in God daily as we are led by the Holy Spirit. Why would you get this serious with God to fight if you are already saved, waiting on heaven, yet believe Jesus already won every battle? This was the deception! Jesus did not leave us here to be sick and destitute. My answer was to be trained for all the others around me. The Holy Spirit was here to teach me all about myself, about us, and how to overcome just as He did with Jesus. Jesus took the Holy

Spirit seriously because He knew the trials and tribulation He would go through. I did not; in fact, I thought He took care of it all for me, which He did. But I did not realize that He and I were to go through my battles together as He did with the Holy Spirit.

I thought I would see the battle coming but I was deceived, and in two blinks of an eye, the battle hit me and changed my life. I don't want anyone to be caught unaware as I was. What happens when the battle is spiritual, but you have lost the ability to depend on your mind, soul, and body to work? What happens when those around you don't understand the battle to help you to fight? In my battle, I started to notice how many sick there were among us in the body of Christ and how much suffering there is. Was the war from atonement's victory supposed to be hidden or cloaked while poverty, bondage, and wickedness are seen? Jesus atoned for all of this. He gave us dominion of the earth and told us to "Follow Him." He told us to go forth and heal the sick, to open the eyes of the blind, set the captives free, and so much more!

I knew it was only by God's grace that I survived the accident, but the pain and loss had only one alternative, and that was for me to wake up and take God seriously. He warns us over and over that the enemy is all around us. Once we see the battle and notice how many people around us suffer, we won't be able to sit still—no, we will have to fight! God tells His people to clear the land of every enemy around us, and I was going to pick off one tree at a time if I had to! The more the enemy came against me, I was determined to take twice as much through prayer from him.

Remembering how merciless the devil was to me inspired me to pray with God in my spirit language for eight hours a day. I could hear the groans of the Spirit within me, and groaning back made me feel better. Still, with so much coming against me, I asked the Holy Spirit how to cut off the wicked. I heard a voice say clearly, **"Stop receiving his gifts!"** Never in all my Christian days did I consider that the devil would bring me a "gift."

I knew every good and perfect gift came from God: these are words of wisdom and knowledge, gifts of faith and healings, miracles, prophecy, speaking in tongues, interpretation of tongues, and the discernment of spirits. There are the virtues of wisdom, knowledge, counsel, fortitude, understanding, piety, and the fear of the Lord. There are also the fruits of the Spirit, which are love, joy, peace, patience, kindness, goodness, gentleness, faith, longsuffering, and self-control, wherewith we see God reflected through our lives. And, there are thousands of God's promises in the Bible to which God responds to us with "yes and amen!" So why was I not clinging daily in the Word with the Holy Spirit to activate all of this? I didn't see my life on this earth as a battle, and during easier times, I was lax with my study and prayer—and this was when I should have been on my knees. The Holy Spirit wanted me to have counsel regarding how Satan counterfeits the gifts of God, so I could know them by their fruits because this was how he was causing chaos in my life.

The enemy has counterfeited love. God is love, and in Him are many benefits with a chastisement to protect us and keep us focused on the Word to finish our race. But not all love that comes into our life is from God, and this can cause so many problems. The enemy likes to use the people who are close to us to hurt us. Look at the effects of his love in our world today. His love does not line up with God's Word, so it causes us to act more like the father of lies than the heavenly Father. The enemy uses people to hurt people, so we do not see the fruit of unity! The Holy Spirit took me through my life and pointed out where I could see how the enemy infected my life, my family, and the body of Christ throughout the history of creation. My healing was never just about me but for all of humanity! This made me able to forgive in a new light because I could see how the enemy's false love turns us outward instead of inward where we belong!

Not understanding the gifts of the enemy was stopping God's love from flowing fully within me and out to others. This was the seedtime and harvest God had spoken so much about in His Word. These seeds of false love were harvesting one generation after the other. These are the roots called "tares" that surrounded the wheat harvest, representing each of us (Matthew 13:24-30). I knew I was commanded to love God and my neighbors as myself. But honestly, how much did I love myself if I took my eternal and physical life for granted? How many times did I treat love as if it was voluntary? I could love my neighbor when I felt like it or get along with people if I was in the mood, but the counterfeit love had attachments to my soul and had left many scars. I could see the enemy's love as the great gulf of distance between the Father looking at the Son covered in my sin on the cross, and this counterfeit was still covering my God-DNA within me. Love was not how my soul wanted to operate, but it should have.

There is something so special when you get to the place where the enemy has kept you blinded and buried, and the Lord of Hosts has finally been allowed to rescue you through His Gift —the Holy Spirit!

What about joy? The joy of the Lord is my strength! The counterfeit gift of joy is misery, despair, sadness, oppression, depression, and even mental illness. I still had much joy because of God and my salvation, but I was also full of the other ungodly gifts. The enemy had been using this counterfeit to steal my whole life. I had to take what I carelessly gave away back, and this time I knew how! I asked the Holy Spirit to train my hands to war, which was to be continuous training. I submitted to God, asking Him to activate the gifts of Him within me. I did not want to look like my enemy. I had to tend to my identity in Jesus Christ. I knew I could only do this by allowing the Word of God to make me an overcomer by the Blood of the Lamb and the word of my testimony. I repented for how carelessly I treated the gifts and fruits of God, but at least now I realized it!

I began to picture the devil as a delivery person who would knock on my door with this big gift, catching my eye just like the fruit in the garden. Had I learned nothing? I saw how the comfort of God I found in my youth had been overtaken with distractions and disappointments, trauma, pain, loss, and grief to the point that they built a fortress around me. I didn't know how to kick these things away from me. Patience was to be grounded in faith that God would meet all of my needs, but I saw myself relying on myself more than on my heavenly Father. The peace of God dwelt within me, but how was I applying His peace to my experience? I was supposed to live in the goodness of God and in the same harmony of the Father, Son, and Holy Spirit. **Do I treat God the way I treat others and myself?** Was I speaking blessing or curses, kindness or selfishness, and what effect would these seeds have on my own life? I think the hardest truth of all was when I meditated on the gift of faith. I thought the opposite of faith was doubt, but I was wrong. The opposite of faith is lack of love! Did I love myself? Did I love myself with God's love?

The enemy's gifts were covering the very DNA of God within me, and this was how he kept me blind. This wasn't a veil; he had me buried! When I started to doubt why the Word wasn't working, fear came to take root, and God was teaching me how the enemy hides and builds strongholds that He wanted out. Deception left me hiding in the very presence of God in disobedience within my soul—and He knew it and still loved me. I wanted the enemy's gifts out! I was done eating in his pastures. The enemy uses such situations to make us think God is a million light-years away from us, but that also is a lie. We are no surprise to God.

Our Father does not turn His back on His kids because we fall and get covered in mud. God is love, and I wanted to know "God love!" The Word of God tells me that I am filled with the knowledge of the will of God in all wisdom and spiritual understanding (Colossians 1:9). God is reflected through me the more I interact with Him.

The Holy Spirit of God is the most gentle Person one could ever encounter. Was I gentle to myself? Honestly, I began to remember when I just wanted all of this mess with the accident over so I could get back to the "normal" routine, but I found my "normal" was truly infected. Why would I fight against God and others, returning evil for evil, instead of fighting with God from His Word to put the defeated enemy to flight? The gift of long-suffering was not about how long God was going to make me suffer before He healed me. True long-suffering means to be forgiving, tolerant, and selfless in obedience to God, doing the Word together as we believe Him. God's example to me of long-suffering was how long He was waiting for me to receive all of His gifts and benefits—and I don't want to make Him wait any longer!

There is something so special when you get to the place where the enemy has kept you blinded and buried, and the Lord of Hosts has finally been allowed to rescue you through His Gift—the Holy Spirit! This is a place of union where we work with God in the Word for the healing of our mind, soul, and memories. This place is where we let God love us right in our saved mess, and we can see all we could have missed. Why was this so life-changing?

Because I was positioned for a miracle. **The place of my defeat was my encounter with Jesus Himself.**

In my worst, filthiest, and ugliest place, He not only loved me more with every breath I took, but He taught me His love! His love is nothing like that of the world. His love is supernatural and made me want to love myself and others the way that He did. When I finally allowed God's love to enter me, He was able to take over my battles. God does not want us wounded, but He knows it is going to happen. When I let God deal with my wounds, I never thought of how I failed or if God was disappointed in me. He was simply waiting for me to let Him love me. God does not want to wait until we are in heaven; He wants all of us now! As my Father, He wanted me to take His every word to my heart so together we could put the enemy to flight. The enemy cracked his whip at my flesh to capture my soul and fill it with deception so I would blame God—and he is still twisting the scriptures just like he did in the Garden of Eden.

When we are in this place, as the enemy comes to defeat us, he no longer sees the weak and blind sheep. Instead, he will meet our Defender face to face! Oh, the love of our Father! God's power through spoken prayer was changing me, and I could see the difference even as I prayed for others. People began to get healed when I prayed for them. The first healing was of hepatitis. The doctor was so shocked that he hung this patient's file on the wall as a reminder to believe! The second miracle was a friend's brother who had stage 4 cancer. He also had reports that the cancer was totally gone from throughout his body. My hunger and faith seeds were bearing fruit. People were getting healed and delivered over the phone through prayer.

I was so proud of God for healing others, but I was not one of them! Every afternoon when the pain was unbearable, I would go back to my bed and cry like a baby! I told Him I would love Him forever even if He didn't heal me—and I meant it! But because Jesus came out of that tomb healed on this earth, there was no way I could not be healed. I could die and go home healed, but He kept me alive! The Scripture says, "With long life I will satisfy him and show him My salvation" (Psalm 91:16 NKJV). Well, I wasn't satisfied, and neither was He! God had miraculously moved, and I knew the next move was mine. I wanted to give God a gift!

God was showing me how miracles are birthed through warfare. I had laid upon my bed so long, envisioning how many people were suffering and how easy it was for God to heal, and I would watch Him in my visions healing one after the other. He wanted me to awaken to a great challenge, and this was to be my gift to Him. My body was not healed yet, but He gave me His strength. I knew I could not accept partial victory ever. I knew if God did not heal or deliver one part of me, and I settled, it would infect my soul and body. The land had to be cleared and every giant removed. I could not get over how much Jesus suffered for all of us to freely receive His many gifts. God never promised that I wouldn't suffer after the cross. He promised He would provide for all I needed and that we would do this together.

Prayer:

Lord, You could have immediately healed me, but I would have remained spiritually disabled and sick. You had to remind me that You are God and You are not like me! I was so infected that my soul did not see it was blind. Thank You for recovering me! I thought I was waiting on my breakthrough, but it was You who was waiting for me. I was to rise through maturing in You by being transformed into Your likeness from glory to glory. You used Your gifts to set me free, which is key to the freedom of others. Your love is not of this world, but Your love through me is desperately needed. My soul was the pit that You pulled me out from. I cannot wait to see what You and I will do next! My healing is not still fully manifested, but I am revived from within. Being obedient in truth, I could see the counterfeit. Keep me awake and on guard to not accept the enemy's gifts but instead with You tell the devil that I reject him with "RETURN TO SENDER!"

Prayer Points

God is overwhelmingly in love with you! Look at your emotions. Are you angry, tired, and misunderstood? Tell God all about it. Record it in a journal and then line up your emotions with a scripture, happy, refreshed, and wisdom from on high. Speak life from your mouth and your ears will believe. Make a recording to play over yourself.

Do your words agree with God for what you are praying and believing for?

During hard times, there's a time to speak and be silent, knowing God has the battle.

Do you love yourself with God's love? Is what God thinks and says about you entering you as truth and light so you can love others with His love?

Chapter 7: The Diagnosis

Chapter 7: The Diagnosis

Twenty-four years after the accident, I was still mostly homebound by pain and meds. Thankfully, I had a really good relationship with my primary care doctor, and he respected my belief that pain medication should be used only to take the edge off of the pain so that a person can endure. I thank God for this gentle and kind man who would listen to me, care for me, and then tell me what he thought we should do next. He respected my fight and the fact that I was not giving in to excessive drugs even as the condition of my body and the level of this pain would bring me daily to my edge. This edge was becoming so sharp that it cut my spirit, soul, and body to the quickness of truth. This blade was like a boundary between what I was going to believe and the illusion I experienced. I was under the weight of the battle yet holding up in my cave, like David waiting and believing the promises of God.

I felt I had submitted so much more of myself that was out of control and took over many areas of my spirit, soul, and body, but I didn't know how to surrender my free will any faster. By this point in my life, I learned that waiting is a huge part of the battle. It became one of the most active things I could do, and I was going to honor God's ability to get me through this while reaping incredible benefits through trusting Him. I remained a daily living sacrifice before the Lord while I was spiritually training and maturing. I was reading the healing Scriptures and watching how people were healed. I was also researching the Bible on how to fight the enemy, who was more than willing to show me that my body couldn't go back to a place of healing. The enemy wanted me to face his facts and believe the reports of the doctors. My flesh would agree with reality, but my soul was strongly battling the pain while agreeing now more with my spirit than the lies of the devil.

My soul was much lighter and clearer, and I was gaining ground, but my mind continued to race and had a hard time staying focused and remembering. The doctors were writing about my disability, and they said that 67% of me was permanently disabled. I could literally hold this fact in my hand, and I was experiencing it every day in my health. The devil encouraged me to just "give up" because I would be so much happier in heaven and pain-free! I reminded him that he was responsible for the pain and sorrow in this world, and I did not agree with him as my forefathers before me. I reminded him that he had no power over me unless I willingly gave it to him, and I was not planning to do that! I also told him that I did not agree with an ungodly belief. It did not matter how I felt or what was written in doctors' reports—his facts didn't agree with the Word of God. In my daily walk with Christ, I was learning that l, too, had a question only I could answer, **"How will I respond."**

God, why do I really follow You?

I also received many of what could be called "small healings," which in themselves were huge: healing in one pain-filled area at a time: healing of a muscle, remembering a Scripture for more than a day, being able to use the bathroom more consistently without laxatives was a huge miracle, and so was being able to get up and move around for three days straight. I still couldn't sleep well because of the pain. Everything I did was scheduled around whether my body would move that day or not. Still, with the adhesions so wrapped around my major organs, I knew I was a walking miracle. The colonoscopy report came back negative, and once again, there were no other options but to open my belly backup to cut me free from them. Even with these miracles, there was so much wrong with me that it might seem that nothing was physically changing. I had learned a very valuable lesson throughout these years: if I saw nothing happening here on the earth, it was absolutely happening in the spirit realm.

No one wanted to cut my belly back open! This time the plan was to cut me north to south instead of east to west to burn and cut these bands off my intestines. The surgeon could not intubate me because my mouth still could barely open, so the plan was five hours of burning and cutting. "Oh God, clear out my garden and plant me afresh and anew with Your seeds of life!" I thought they could have removed them all in five hours, but only one area was released—and to recover after this surgery, I wasn't allowed to lift anything heavier than five pounds and no pulling or exercise. My body seemed to be treating my existence as a parasite. The inside of me was actually much worse than the outside. I had to put everything I used on the counters to not have to pull open a drawer. My house looked as good as my inner self. Every day of my existence showed my choice of whose side I was on. God's side required perfect trust in Him, but I really wanted healing right that moment! I had to remind myself daily that we had a relationship based on agreement, and God wanted my faith mixed with endurance. My life was no longer my own—but His.

Some days I felt like the Israelites in the Bible. They were freed from the harsh bondage they were used to and saw the miracles of God as He delivered them. I also was freed from bondage that I didn't even realize I was in, bondage that kept me in disobedience to God. I, too, had seen many miracles. For instance, after my first and second facial reconstruction surgeries, I had migraine headaches almost daily for ten straight years. They were so horrible that I could hear the pounding in my head like deafening drums. I had to take strong medicine to bear that pain and many times had to remain in the dark. I could not read the Word in the dark but found great comfort there with my eyes closed, knowing God was with me. I was learning the difference between mental peace and spiritual peace. Spiritual peace is not focused on my emotions but on Jesus.

The Diagnosis

One day I had a vision of very bright light, and I knew it was God. I could not see His face but a bright light upon what looked like a throne. All I could say to my heavenly Father was, "God, can You turn it down a little?" I covered my eyes, but He was still there. I heard these words in my heart, "Pegge, do you think I AM sitting up here on My throne with a migraine headache?" "Of course not," I replied. He said, "Do you live and move and breathe in Me?" "Yes, God, and You know that is one of my favorite Scriptures!" He replied, "If you live in Me, then how could you have a migraine?" I received His Word! When the vision was gone, so was the migraine! From that day, I never had another migraine headache. Yes, I tried this with the rest of my afflictions but learned thankfulness not to have to sit in the darkness.

Just like the Israelites who received wealth from the Egyptians, I also saw a wealth transfer. The doctors told me that I needed to sell my farm because what wasn't broken in me would be if I continued farming. I was infuriated and afraid, thinking, "Who do they think they are?" This was the only income that I had to pay for the accident from the man who had no insurance and owned nothing that I had already forgiven. I even brought it to God in prayer, thinking He would agree with me against this. This was an idol in my heart that I brought before God, thinking what I wanted was more important than Him. And, honestly, I didn't want to hear what He had to say because I could not fathom that He would agree with the doctors, so I waited. I had to place the farm and my income on the altar of sacrifice, and after many days I brought the farm before the Lord. He said that He no longer wanted me to tend His animals. He wanted me to tend to His people. Still, from pride, disbelief, and every emotion He knew I was dealing with, I asked Him for a fleece to confirm His words to me. **I asked Him for the impossible.** I said if He would sell the farm in one week that I knew it was Him. I had a down payment on day three! I chose to submit and cooperate, and after using the money from the sale to pay for a place to live, the surgeries, doctor bills, meds, and everything else, I had to go on state aid. I went from wealthy to welfare and I have to testify that God still faithfully paid my bills. On this small amount of money, I knew that if I tithed, He would be faithful. One day I had to ask God how I would retire, losing all my income at such a young age, and He so calmly assured me that I had the best retirement plan there is! Selah! I saw so many financial miracles during these years. Even while lying on my bed, I started believing Him for my retirement.

It was so easy for me to ask God to do what I thought was impossible with the farm because I didn't think He would do it, yet such a struggle for my healing which I believed He would do. In Psalm 23 (NKJV), we read, "The Lord is my Shepherd; I shall not want. **He makes me to lie down** in green pastures," And right here I received the revelation of "my diagnosis." My free will had been resisting Him. Oh, I knew how to make a sheep lie down. You have to sneak up behind it, grab both of its back legs and hold on tight! The sheep's front legs will keep running, but the shepherd must carefully hold those legs and then twist the body of that sheep onto its back because when a sheep is on its back, it can't do anything. This is exactly where I was. I was being made to lay down by my Shepherd in green pastures in His presence, and while there, He fed me with His living water because His goal was to restore my soul. Oh, what a revelation! Again, I vowed my love to my beloved Shepherd.

His love was not about performance but relationship.

My "sheep" life was under the Shepherd's care but was centered on me and my way of operating instead of obedience to my beloved Shepherd. God Himself would call me deeper into His Word and into Him every day, but many times I responded with my multiple excuses just like the Shulamite (Song of Songs 5:2-8). And because of my experience with this horrible accident, I realized that all my excuses were in every book of the Bible. "God, I have a business to run; God I have a field to plow; God, I have to teach children's church; God, I went to church, so now I'll watch TV instead of reading Your Word, and even, "God, I'm broken. All I can do is lie here!" Okay, I added a couple, but seriously, I was in the Word, I loved God, and I was serious about doing good, knowing there was no true "good" in me except Him. But to come under the shadow of the Most High, I needed to dwell with the person of God in a daily relationship. This was coming into union with the love of God Himself

"God, why do I really follow You?" Had I become like the people of Jesus' hometown who were so familiar with Him without knowing Him personally? Was my motive to follow Him because He freely fed? His love was not about performance but relationship. **I wasn't supposed to understand God but follow Him with pure trust!** The Israelites watched God open the Sea so they could walk over in sandals on dry ground. They had a cloud that guided them by day and a tornado of fire that stayed with them by night. This was God's tangible presence, but their newfound freedom was not what they were expecting. I also had God's presence and received miracles and watched God heal others, but my freedom was not what I was expecting. Seeing the power of God was not enough!

I firmly believe that the people in the Bible represent each season of our lives. I found myself acting just like them. **I wondered if God wanted to heal everyone else but me.** The Father did not spare the Son. Was this my cup to drink? I knew it was a miracle just to endure this indescribable pain day after day. The Israelites had seen both the standoff between God and Pharaoh and God's amazing miracles. I was watching the standoff between God and my diagnosis, and there were some days when I thought God was hardening my enemy against me because the diagnosis was getting longer and not shorter. There I was with God telling me that He was crossing me into the Promised Land. Sometimes I wondered if I had to wait for forty years, too, just like the Israelites did until they finally reached their destination.

All the miracles they saw did not bring them faith!

Even after the miracles of Egypt were over and the wilderness experience was behind them, the Promised Land wasn't a piece of cake. "Why does everything have to be so hard, God?" He answered in a still small voice, **"What do you think it was like for My Son?"** This Suffering Servant is my hero! Every time I was brought back to His suffering, I was encouraged! Oh, how I longed to have a list of all the wonderful things God had done in my life. I wanted each wonder written upon a string of pearls I could wear around my neck to read and praise Him for all of His kindness! I wanted to thank Him for everything and understand His nature as He was uniting me with His divine faith. I was now looking back, still living in His divine blessings, watching how my faith had matured as I believed God because He is God.

My diagnosis was a giant that needed to be terminated! I was also a giant of self, and I had no idea how powerful this self-will is until I watched it bully me. God's people did not want to deal with the slaying of these giants either, but this was their way to the Promised Land. Yet even in the Promised Land, with the great progress being made and the power of God available for an instant miracle, a sign or a wonder was not enough. The giants had walled cities, and God's people had tents. How much spiritual warfare did they know? They had God right there with them, but how would they respond? I saw Joshua and Caleb as Jesus and the Holy Spirit. (See Numbers 13:16-33 for Joshua and Caleb's story.) The other ten men never once mentioned God—only their circumstances, their fear, and doubt. When they believed they could not overcome the giants, they revolted against Moses, Joshua, and Caleb.

God taught me so much about the living power in my soul and how it can revolt and lead us down the wrong path. All the miracles they saw did not bring them faith. Faith does not come from miracles! Faith comes by hearing and responding to the Word of God. God told me to live in Him from His Word bearing living faith because He was preparing me for miracles, as He told me to "go" even while I could barely move. Even though this was His command, **I still had to make a choice,** and I was not going to deny Him! God taught me to look into each Bible story with the Holy Spirit and watch as each story came to life. This made the Word and my faith alive. The Holy Spirit deeply awakened me so the Word could live in my heart— even in my much-damaged temple.

I began to think about how other believers responded to their battles. I knew a great cloud of witnesses gave their all under terrible persecution, torture, and death. I thought of Christians being persecuted just because they believe in God and how many others are starving, abused, in prison, or worse yet, living without a Bible. How many were sick and in pain with no medical help? I would pray for all of these as if my life depended on it. My motive was based on my thought of wondering if the body of Christ was praying for me. After two decades, I had seen many fall away from the battle that was no longer praying for me or even caring about me, and this was teaching me to never give up as each one of us is a precious treasure in the eyes of God. Thinking of how those with mental illnesses, blindness, deafness, muteness, and those who cared for them also suffer would help me realize that we are one body and that we should never leave our wounded on the battlefield.

The Diagnosis

Each word of my prayers became seeds for healing, deliverance, restoration, and blessing—and I was sowing seeds in others for my own healing.

I had to close my eyes; I had to close my ears. I had to just dwell in His presence and take the pain and the reports deeper into the intimacy of His suffering. God was training me through prayer in this place to manifest healing from heaven into my life and the lives of others. It is amazing that in the depths of suffering, we are willing to do so much for others while we lose sight of ourselves. God brought me to a place deep within me where I believed I was not worth it all, and I believe this was the deepest root hidden in my soul that God was aiming for all this time. I had been hurt so much that even as a young lady, this root had formed and was fed by the enemy's lies. I had heard so many horrible words over me and suffered so much that deep within me, I thought I was different, and since I suffered much at the hands of those I loved, I began to believe these words as facts and religion backed them up.

My deepest deception was rooted in the fact that even as a young girl, I felt I was too broken to fix, and here as an adult, I manifested my belief. God wanted me here in this place with Him, and it was so uncomfortable because it was the place where even the impossible was possible with Him. I needed God to change the entire diagnosis. He showed me more of who I truly am and anointed me to remove these graveclothes I had carried through my life. I wanted His godly garments to cover my soul. I thought I had dealt with this a long time ago. I thought I had been delivered and forgave all, but there were scars, and God had come to remove them one after the other. He was coming for a bride, and He was removing my "wrinkles," and I had no idea that I had them until I saw the wounds and scars I carried—and I'm not talking about scars from my accident (Ephesians 5:26-27).

I asked God why I was suffering so much. He said I was being clothed in His Son! I asked if this was to lift my head and remove all the shame I carried from my past. He said my old life was removed, and I am already a new creation! I had to submit to how much God loved me in places within me that no love had been allowed, and I received His grace and freedom. I continued to ask God, "What else am I hiding in Your presence?" To this day, this is one of my continual questions to God. This was now a weight that I was never meant to carry and a hindrance I could no longer allow. If my trials were uncovering the old me, I wanted total resurrection with Jesus. As I responded to God's diagnosis, I was allowed to see how my past was holding me back from revealing abundant living to myself and my family. My past died with Christ, but I was now paying attention to how my soul—the thoughts, motives, and deeds of my mind and heart—were responding to the kingdom of heaven. The Holy Spirit was training me on how to live in the kingdom, and I wanted to be a holy vessel for the Holy Spirit. I wanted to follow Jesus and finish well! I was being transformed. How will I behave, trust God, and act in heaven? I am practicing now!

I had been on high dosages of water pills to help pull swelling from my body. Decades after the accident, my back muscles were full of knots and swelling. And even though I thought I was feeling better, the latest CT scan showed that both of my kidneys were covered with cysts. I also had gallstones, and my surgeon wanted to remove my gallbladder because I was having attacks and pain. The doctors also said that I could no longer have cortisone shots in my spine to relieve the pain, and yet in all of this, I had another miracle!

One night I had a dream from the Lord about my brain. He said that my brain had been damaged in the accident, but the doctors never checked why I was still having so many problems with my thoughts racing and then forgetting. I told my doctor I wanted to have my brain checked, and he sent me to a psychologist. The psychologist knew exactly what the problem was. He did his testing and diagnosed me with adult ADHD. He said that it wasn't a mental thing as much as a damage thing and that my brain had suffered considerable trauma when my face was crushed by the steering wheel. I had no idea that traumatic brain injury was linked to the symptoms of ADHD, but God did! After decades of being tormented, I received my answer through a dream that it was medical, so I stopped blaming myself and joyfully repented because I was so grateful to God! I knew that this would also be temporary as I prayed for Jesus to heal my brain. The psychologist said that it was so bad that he prescribed a large dose of amphetamine to calm me down. Praise God, it worked!

I was amazed why this drug worked! I didn't like pills or an additional diagnosis, but I had peace and clarity of mind. I could only find comfort that this would also bring a greater testimony. However, my new peace of mind brought additional problems. My body could not handle any additional weight. The steroids that had been injected into my spine for so long had caused swelling in my face and hands, and this was not helping my mouth to open. The amphetamine usually would make people lose weight, especially in high doses, but for some reason, medicine had an opposite effect on me. Between the medications and the amphetamines, I gained an additional sixty pounds. I had been trying to watch my weight to take the stress from my back and joints. The water pills to remove the swelling in my body would remove the excess fluid but drain out my potassium, which could cause heart failure. The adhesions controlled what, when, or if I was eating, and the amphetamine left me only hungry at night where I wanted a big meal before bed. The doctor offered me sleeping pills, and when he said they would knock me out, I knew better. The enemy was trying so hard to kill me, but God wanted me alive so I could know without a doubt that nothing is impossible with Him, that I am already healed, and that I am more than a conqueror.

When would I finally stop with my own diagnosis of what I wanted in life?

But, in all seriousness, what was God's plan for my life? He knew all about the people who hurt me, and He taught me to forgive and love them. He knew all about the accident and all it would do to my life. God trained me throughout this process to watch and recognize my enemy, his tricks, seeds, and patterns. I was a formidable foe, and I had no idea how I truly operated from my depths within. Yet, God said His plan for me was good, and I began to imagine what His plan was. I knew the plan was in His timing, and I believed I was now submitting and cooperating in all of this so that He would give me the desires of my heart. What are they? Only God knew. It is the glory of God to conceal a matter, but the honor of kings to search out and discover them.

I had just finished my associate's degree right before the accident happened. Yet, throughout all this suffering, there were three prophetic words over me I could not forget. They were alive in my heart, and I knew without a doubt that God said I would finish my education. My Father was training me to watch how He fulfills the desires of my heart—which are actually His desires for me. God led me to start a home business raising a beautiful breed of small dogs, and all of my education was paid for through this income. It was a profound miracle for me to finish my BA degree in social sciences because so much time passed since the accident that I had to start over from the beginning. Sitting and studying was another challenge for my lower spine; it was still the worst pain in my body. I believed I was obeying the Lord and completed by His grace even my master's degree through Christian Leadership University, which is focused on hearing the voice of God. Still, His path left me totally dependent on Him for my income!

I pushed through school, struggling to be able to sit longer than twenty minutes. I enjoyed all the reading and deadlines because I was always business-oriented and felt I was regaining life! Throughout this experience, I had been pleading with God over two things: First of all, I wanted to go back to work! I wanted to make a "living," but He wanted me to make a "giving." God knew my driving motive of getting through school was to go back to work or start a business. I knew that I was not in agreement with Him, and He had no problem and with such love and kindness to bring this to my attention. Not working cut into every ethical belief I had! I was so stubborn that I wanted to get a job in between surgeries, being hardly able to move!

One day as I looked through the employment section of the paper, I saw a legal secretary position with good pay and benefits. Somewhere within me, I believed all this would end if I just went back to work. So I called the ad, and the lawyer's wife answered the phone. She was filling in until they hired someone. I told her my ten years of experience, and she said, "You're hired!" She wanted me to come in to fill out my paperwork and start the next Monday. I got to the car and barely got down the road when my phone rang, and it was a conference call. Two of my friends, one a missionary in China, had called a dear local sister in Christ to get me on the phone to ask me a question, **"Where do you think you are going?** God told them to tell me, "Turn around and go home!" I had to humble myself and call the woman and quit before I could start. When would I finally stop with my own diagnosis of what I wanted in life, and how easy was it for God to have someone in China tell me?

The second thing I pleaded with God about was that He wanted me to become a pastor! This was not something I chose, but God chose for me. Living in my body did not inspire accountability before God for the care of His people? God told me before the accident that I would be a Christian counselor and that I am His church. As a pastor, I was allowed into the hospitals to pray with people who needed a touch from the Lord. God kept telling me I could counsel from home and that He would send me His people! All the power of God Almighty kept me in check through His gentleness while humble in Spirit. He said the yoke He would give me was easy, and the load He would put on me was light (Matthew 11:28-30). Oh, the love of God was absolutely killing the plans I had even after my healing. Giving Him my life was not in word only. The third word was that He and I would minister together, and we did this throughout my whole ordeal!

I embraced the call of God! I was to serve Him, and with myself out of the way, I would just hold His hand on the journey. God told me this is exactly what I wanted with Him. I just knew I could not miss what God has planned for me to do on this earth, and I no longer want to be healed just so I could live for myself. No, I want Him to live through me! It was so hard to just be still and know that He is God while I would struggle, stop and grow every step of the way. He already healed me, but my faith was growing faith upon faith. This was my personal agony of dying to self, carrying my cross, and resurrecting with Him daily. I was following Him and learning how to live as a citizen of heaven now! I believed in God but also had faith in myself, and this was my diagnosis to Him. I told Him I was exhausted. I knew He would love me like no other and found great comfort in knowing He would keep me full of Him on the straight and narrow as He looked over my spirit and soul.

Prayer:

Father, Jesus taught me how to read a diagnosis. When the devil brings up my past, I tell him we left that in the pit. It is not who I am, for I am a new creation that is made new every day. I live in You! When the doctor's reports get longer and longer, Your faith dwelling in mine will bring joy every morning! When I feel the pain and cannot function, I ask You to overtake all as I am being transformed into Your very image and likeness, and I know You believe. When I do not understand and am so absolutely frustrated, You patiently bring spiritual understanding with knowledge that frees me from within.

Father, thank You for teaching me how to speak the language of heaven and how to believe beyond what I think or could imagine. In the lowest of all my lowest places, You remain so close. I can see the process of heaven on earth, and You are my greatest encourager! You did not allow this to happen, but You surely are using this to turn every issue into a mountain of possibilities.

Prayer Points

What are you going through? Look at the illusion of the problem and speak faith over it.

Waiting is a huge part of the battle. How will you respond—with God or without Him?

If you see nothing happening on the earth when you pray, know that it is absolutely being dealt with in the spiritual realm.

We are not supposed to understand God, but follow Him and trust Him. What questions can you leave with Him that you have no answer for?

God, what am I trying to hide from Your presence?

What is the diagnosis you have of your life? Is it God's desire and plan for you, or your own?

Chapter 8: The Final Fight

Chapter 8: The Final Fight

I came to a place where time itself no longer had the same meaning. All of my waiting on God transformed me into His realm, where time meant nothing more than abiding with Him! It was now twenty-six years since the accident. I believed the first doctors diagnosis that my muscles would be sore for a few weeks and resisted the specialists' evidence, even though I could visibly see and experience all they reported. Man could not heal what God had created. Only the Great Physician could do that! God had so much more for me, and in Him, I was already loved and whole. I did not want to be "devoted" but "united." I wanted to live as a citizen of heaven while on earth. I had no control over what I once called "my life," and I was living day by day only by the breath and grace of God. God's definition of time took everything I did without Him out of view. Time was changed to patience, and God's patience was so perfect compared to what I had been taught. My suffering allowed me to touch the intimacy of Jesus' suffering, and through this, I had His focus on the affliction and pain still experienced in the body of Christ.

There were so many forms of suffering found in the Bible, yet the perfect form of suffering did not involve avoidance; instead, Jesus was preparing Himself to press forward in it with joy. Just like Him, my soul had to be trained by the Holy Spirit. I wanted to love God with my whole heart, soul, mind, and strength, but I had no idea what it would mean for me to come into union with God through yielding and agreeing. I was created to be a vessel for Him, full of Him to continue the work of "God with us" on the earth. There were so many stages within my suffering that through transformation came a deeper flow of Him in me and I in Him. When I was weak, His strength would flow through me. When I wanted immediate healing, I would surrender every area of pain back to Him. I could sense His compassion flowing, and it would take me into prayer to join my compassion with His, interceding for His people. Every time I thought of doing my life my way, I sacrificed it all back to God. God wanted to unite His supernatural life in mine!

My Father also knew that I would have to go through three additional lysis of adhesions surgeries to continue burning and cutting out these bands of scar tissue that inhabited my inward parts. The surgeon again explained to me that these bands resembled a plastic covering my organs like a strong adhesive. I thought most of the adhesions were around my lower intestines area until they had to remove my gallbladder. The surgeon found it was also covered in adhesions.

The enemy wanted me to believe that he had won!

Fear threatened to grip me thinking of how extensive the adhesions could be, remembering the surgeries on my face, neck, shoulder, and ribs, but instead of surrendering to this feeling, I prayed for God to keep the adhesions away from my heart. I continued praying the adhesions would be supernaturally removed. Honestly, I felt these "roots" within me were like a forest, and Jesus and I had to remove this giant from my land. Still, I didn't know what else to do but pray, believe, and stand on the Word of God. I believed my answer would be brought forth out of praying in my spirit language, knowing prayer and praise were weapons that manifested change. Meanwhile, the doctors kept me on the fluid pills to eliminate the unneeded water and salt from my kidneys and aid my heart. I could only hope and pray that my heart would not be affected by these meds, and by the grace of God, it wasn't.

My core body temperature was dropping, and I didn't know why. I would suddenly feel bone-chilling cold, take my temperature, and find it was 94 or 95 degrees. Another giant! The doctor put me on thyroid meds, which changed nothing. I sought the Lord again and began another journey of learning more about my body. But with all the additional weight and all the new drugs and diagnosis, my limbs became problematic. My knee had suffered greatly in the accident, but it wasn't until years later that the damage took its toll. The doctors would keep inserting needles into my knee to drain the fluid. I was so tired of surgeries, doctors, and needles, but I was surrendering to "whatever God's plan was." I could only keep seeking how He wanted me to respond. The enemy continued to pound on me, and I continued to fight every doubt. Many times my only prayer was my tears, but I knew Jesus understood. My right knee had already survived through one surgery, but the wear and tear continued.

Two years after that operation, the swelling returned, and the surgeon confirmed that the meniscus had torn. I kept praying and believing for God to deliver me from another knee surgery while suffering from pain and swelling. I knew by now that if one part of the body was not working at full capacity, it affected the rest of me, like the way I was walking was affecting my back and hips. I remember one Sunday morning when my right knee was the size of my thigh. I wanted to go to church, but my knee was so hot to the touch. Guess what I heard: God said, "Go to church!" I responded, "Yes, Lord!"

I looked awful from the many sleepless nights, and I wasn't sure if I could even press the gas pedal or how I would bend my leg to get into the car. I couldn't doubt the command because I knew it was Him. I threw a dress over my head and believed if He wanted me to go to church that He would get me in and out of the car. I prayed in agony, dried my face, and hobbled into church. I made it to the last pew. The worship began, and I was so thankful to be there that all of me, my spirit, soul, mind, strength, and body were rejoicing. I stood behind the pew to hold on and thanked God for His constant care of me. I was doing a "victory dance" from within my temple. I let go of the pew to raise my hands to God, and His power and presence fell on me like a cloud. I thought it had to have been a rain cloud because I could feel my tears running off my chin, and immediately as God inhabited my praise, the swelling left my knee! I was a mess! I was crying and rejoicing out loud! I had my own miracle service in the back of the church. I walked to the front and gave my testimony to give God all the glory! But, one year later, I had to have a second surgery.

How can this be God? You sovereignly healed my knee that day! How could this happen again? My body was created to heal itself year by year if I took care of my health. **The enemy wanted me to believe that he had won.** He wanted me to believe that it was just too much to recover. And after the knee surgery and more rehabilitation, I was back to walking my only remaining little dog. He saw a squirrel, and when he pulled me, I heard and felt my right shoulder tear. I was petrified. All the surgeries I had gone through left me believing I could never go through such pain again. It was only by the grace of God that I survived horrible double facial reconstruction surgeries, and when the doctors removed the muscles from my neck, they honestly warned me that could leave me paralyzed; still, nothing was as frightening as the shoulder. I believed I had lost my tolerance for pain with the left shoulder reconstruction. "God, have mercy on me, Lord! Heal me!" I cried. I heard the Lord say peacefully, **"I already have healed you!"** I believed Him and responded, "I know, God, and I believe that my healing has already taken place. I am just waiting on my body to catch up with my belief." Just the thought of not using my right arm was debilitating. This tear had me so determined to take care of myself, and I knew the enemy wanted me to believe that God had given me more than I could handle. I was becoming more determined than ever to take care of myself. I was careful and very specific in fasting and prayer. I had planted a small garden using plastic to prevent weeds, and even though I would be so sore afterward, I enjoyed working the land. I had also begun dehydrating my own food so I would eat healthy on the days I could not cook.

Each battle was as unique as I was.

By this time, I had completed my master's degree and had become a pastor. I was doing counseling within the church I attended when I was able. So much progress— and still such a test for my faith! I kept looking at that tomb door in my mind and saw my healed self walking out. The degeneration in my spine was becoming worse, and I could no longer care for my little dog. My lower back had always been the most painful part of my body, and to make it worse, six to eight times every year, I would get shingles in this same area. They are a reactivation of the chickenpox virus I had as a child causing a blistering painful rash as it ran on the nerve tissues in my lower back and near my spinal cord. The doctors would offer me more pain medicine to help me, but it was not helping, so I refused.

The Final Fight

There was a surgeon in North Carolina who believed the best way to get me off the pain meds was to cut off the bottom of my spine, but "there were many risks." How could I cut off the bottom of my spine? A coccygectomy surgery has shown to relieve pain, which sounded like heaven touching earth to me, but could I dare to take the chance of adhesions forming around the nerves of my spine? And, I already had so many MRIs and CT scans that it would have to be super important to subject me to more radiation. I said, "No, God gave me my spine, and I am keeping it. God healed me, and I am waiting on my spine to believe."

What didn't make sense to me was the amount of daily pain I was in while my body was healing and improving. If you looked at me, you would never imagine how much damage was on my insides. I knew my authority in Christ, and I gave my heart instructions to meditate on whatever verse came to light. I commanded my emotions to battle against the flesh, and I demanded every enemy spirit to come out and loose its hold. I commanded my body to be healed nerve by nerve and precept by precept. I spoke life into my muscles, one muscle at a time. Every mistake I made, either through pain or confession, ultimately led me closer to God. I used to say that God has even anointed my mistakes to prosper, bringing me deeper into union with Him. Each battle was as unique as I was. I had to be taught what was personal and what included the entire body of Christ. I had to learn to wait on the Holy Spirit to allow me in the battle or rest in Him and not be involved. I had to learn and repeatedly practice my spiritual response to the situation and not respond with my mind, soul, or flesh because if I allowed it to rage, my muscles would tighten up, causing more pain. I failed uncountable times, but God was not upset with me, and training would continue.

I kept my journals. Most of my days and nights are recorded. Some are legible, and some are not. Just peeking through some for my testimony reminded me that most were written and never looked upon again. I was rejoicing while briefly reading through my notes because God has answered my prayers. I praise God that I kept a record of the so many things He has brought me through. As I was crying out for myself and others in pain and prayer, the Lord responded in His calm, soft voice: "**Pegge, are you tired of your pain?**" Yes, I was! Then He said, "Let My wrath touch your pain and tell it to leave you" (Psalm 138:7). I could feel it flowing through me, and with a burst of power from within me, I commanded the pain to leave me and instead be placed on the enemy. The Lord said that vengeance is His, but I was absolutely up to sharing His vengeance on our enemy. God taught me how to release His punishment from heaven to the offense and crimes done against me by the enemy, and I was honored to share with God as He divinely chastised those that trespassed against me.

Finally, twenty-nine years after the accident, the day came when my doctor told me to go again to the surgeon and seek him for another additional lysis of adhesions surgery. I remember telling my doctor, "He is not going to touch me with a ten-foot pole," and my doctor said, "You are absolutely right, Pegge, but I need you to go to the surgeon, and I need you to hear this for yourself." So I went. He opened my file, looked up at me, and said, "Oh,

I remember you! I took pictures of your belly the last time and sent them to the New England Journal of Medicine. I won't touch you with a ten-foot pole! And I guarantee you there is not another surgeon who will either." He said, "Look, we will give you all the pain medicine you need. Just go home and die! There is nothing else we can do for you."

I so wished I had my phone recorder on because I was not ready to hear the word *die*! He wrote in my medical record, "Patient was told there was no need for surgery now but recommended for her to return if conditions worsened." I knew he was telling me what he believed to be the truth, and I remember walking out of his office and looking up at the sky, saying, "God, did You hear what he said? If my body doesn't line up now, he says it will die, and I know You are going to finish what You started." I felt as though Goliath was taunting my God! Something happened to me in that very instant. I felt so much hope flowing inside of me because man and I had finally run out of knowledge of doing things. And as I got in the car, I remember saying to God, "I am finally in the perfect place for a miracle!" So I went home, and I prayed my daily prayer, "God, what do You want me to do?" And I sensed in my spirit God saying, "I want you to go on YouTube and watch miracles, signs, and wonders!"

I had watched teaching after teaching on YouTube, but I had no idea that YouTube had miracles, signs, and wonders, but I obeyed the Master, and behold, there were videos of miracles, signs, and wonders on YouTube! I remember scrolling down the list and feeling the Holy

Spirit stop me at a certain ministry. I sensed God wanting me to sit under the particular ministry and was instructed to watch the videos for a period of one year! I remember one day when I watched a deliverance video and literally felt a lying spirit leave my body. God was conquering every lie I had believed and allowed to dwell within me. Deliverance was something God had flowed through in me for decades and was continually training me in during my recovery, but when I felt that demon leave, I knew God had made such progress in me that I could see the demonic so much clearer and experience such joy watching them get kicked out! My heavenly Father had birthed so much ministry and gifting while I was trained upon my bed. He was going to use me online and touch His people.

It came to the point where I sensed God telling me not to put a pill in my mouth until I spoke out my two pages of healing Scriptures. I even prayed over the medication. The Word of God was medicine from heaven. I would say, "Father, I ask You to take everything in the world, every plan of the enemy out of each one of these tablets and capsules, and I ask You to fill it with Your food, Your water, Your vitamins, and Your minerals from heaven because You are my Healer!" I would speak my Scripture medicine as loud as I could three times a day. Why was this important? Because I needed to hear the Word of God over everything else that the doctors said that I had believed and that the enemy was trying to lie to me about. I was still battling pain and still commanding it to get out. The pain was now my reminder to act upon the Word. I had noticed that the pain would become unbearable around 4 p.m. How could pain tell time? I realized the accident happened around 4 p.m. and I began to forgive everything and pray into 4 o'clock! Now, God told me to do all of this right from the beginning, but I was not strong enough. I relied on my strength when God wanted me to draw from His strength.

God wanted my testimony!

Going from a place of disability to a place of hope was amazing! Miracles had now become a part of my everyday life. I knew that if God spoke His Word, it would happen. This was the God I believed in as a young girl! This was the God I believed in all my life! This was my loving Father I conversed with every day, listening to the Bible app. This was the Great I Am I knew was surrounding me every single day! Seeing people sick was now out of order for me. Seeing people suffering, being demonized, or oppressed was not acceptable. Miracles, signs, and wonders became "normal" to me, and I knew I had my answer as I saw all that was birthed through my waiting in Him.

I heard the Lord telling me to pray for that certain ministry to come to the United States! One day I found out that they were coming, but it would be months before they arrived. Meanwhile, the people I prayed for continued being healed and delivered. I was still serving people through counseling and praying for them on the phone. If a person was "incurable," I could feel the joy of the Lord rise within me, and many He would instantly heal. He healed so many—but not me!

When it finally came to the week when the minister would be doing a meeting in the state next to mine, the pain was worse than ever. I sensed the Lord asking if I was going to the meeting. I replied, "Lord, I don't think I can sit three-and-a-half hours one way to make it to this meeting." So He placed on my heart this one client who had suffered so horribly throughout her lifetime. God had delivered her of so much demonic oppression, but she still was bound by a horrible childhood. This demon had kept her in psych wards most of her life, and there was one stronghold she refused to release to God. She told me she was going to move and that this was our last session. I felt in my heart that the greatest gift that I could give to this girl was to drive her to this meeting. So I mentioned what I was going to do, and other people wanted to come too. We rented the largest van we could find, filled it up with the people I knew were in the most need, and drove to the meeting.

The ride there was absolutely horrible! First, my pain was at its worst. Then the people in the van were manifesting and arguing. To me, this was a sign we were all getting healed, and the enemy knew it! My friend took over driving because the pain was so unbearable. I had to take the pain meds, and as I took the bottles out of my purse, I said, "Tonight is your last night!" Then I had a word for the devil, "Devil, tonight is your last night. I know that tonight Jesus has and is going to recover me." The more everyone in the van kept arguing, the more I continued to push into my healing. I told them all, "Ladies, even the devil knows I am going to get healed tonight!" I tuned out the noise. I could not afford to be distracted by time, pain, people, or manifesting demons. I immediately had a vision. I saw the meeting room full of people, and I saw the minister. I knew from the vision that even if this anointed man did not pray for me that I was walking out to the van absolutely healed and free! My eyes were on Jesus, and in the vision, I watched the Great I Am moving right through my body like a wind of fire. Then I heard Him say these words, "This one is Mine!" God had all my bases covered—right down to any fear creeping in that something could go wrong. I was going to have a divine encounter with the Great Physician!

When we got to the meeting and worship started, I felt the move of the Holy Spirit throughout the room. There was so much peace within me, and I knew that I was being healed during worship even before the meeting started. I knew when the minister began that he would pray for the people that were first located by the Holy Spirit. As he did, they fell on the floor. He had words of knowledge for them, and it witnessed to their spirits. Many got up and testified their pain was gone or their mental anguish had ceased, and I was watching the presence of God all around me. I knew from watching the videos for over a year that my time was now, and I had "**NOW FAITH**" and "**NOW WAS THE ACCEPTABLE TIME!**" I also knew that the Holy Spirit would only locate a few people, and then there would be a prayer line for the rest. So I said again, "God, even if this man does not pray for me, I already know YOU ARE GOING TO HEAL ME! I have already seen the end of the vision!"

I believed God's report!

Everything I had been through in those thirty years was all spiritually visible during worship, and I was ready to let it all go. I kept thinking of Jesus coming out of that tomb alive, scarred and healed before He resurrected into heaven. I was going to walk out of this mess healed while I was still alive, scarred; and I was going to finish what God had destined for me to do. I was the last person who was located by the Holy Spirit. I stood up, and the minister asked me what I wanted Jesus to do for me. I briefly told him because I knew the Holy Spirit knew everything about me, and I wanted to be quiet so he could receive instructions from the Holy Spirit. The healing power of God entered me in a moment so powerful I could only be having an encounter with the Living God. I had already experienced many encounters with Jesus, but now My Dad, the Ancient of Days, had come to rescue His child. I felt a fire burning in my abdomen, and I felt like a tree growing up into my spine, and muscles were forming like leaves on the tree on both sides of it. Somehow, I was still able to stand on my feet in such a strong presence of Almighty God.

The minister saw that God was giving me a new stomach and new discs. He saw that my major organs were only alive and working by the Word and grace of God! But all I could feel was my back, my muscles, my nerves, and my neck being touched by God. Even the minister was amazed at the power of God flowing through me. He said to the people, "There is a gentle touch of God, and then there is the resurrection power of God. What we are seeing is the 'Ancient of Days' at work!" Then I fell on the floor, and while I was down on the floor, God had this minister see the condition of my tailbone. The Lord had him specifically speak the words that I most needed to hear. This minister watched God as my new spine, and my new tailbone became perfectly aligned. And as if all of this was not enough, the minister said that he saw Jesus standing right near my feet. And Jesus was speaking a word that came forth from His mouth like thunder as He said: **"This one is Mine!"** And with that, it was over.

In that five minutes, I had a meeting with God Himself, and while I was still on the floor and the meeting continued around me, I heard the Lord say to me, "Now, I AM sending you out into full-time ministry." I laid there soaking in the Lord, thanking Him for all He had done. When I got up, I knew that I was healed! I was so healed that I was going to finish the vision and go out the door, get in the van, and go home! I thanked God that I had come out of the tomb! I was alive, and all the pain was absolutely gone! The miracle was so complete that I already forgot what it was like to be in pain. I went into the bathroom to press my body. No pain.

As I was heading for the van I heard the Lord say, "NO! I want your testimony!" Right then, someone from the ministry team came and said the minister wanted to talk with me. I was so proud to walk to the front with no pain to glorify my Dad! I kept saying with each step, "I knew You would do it! I knew You would do it!" I gave my testimony, and I thanked the minister for standing in faith with me. I had strong faith, but I needed somebody that would stand in strong faith with me. I also shared about the vision in which God said, "This one is Mine!" The minister told me that the night before the meeting, the prayer helpers prayed with him for all who would be harassed by the enemy or were in so much pain that they didn't think they could make it to the meeting! As he was speaking, I watched as God etched that prayer in my heart to pray for others. God wanted me to stand in faith for others! My healing was recorded on video for the glory of God!

As I walked to the van and opened the door, I heard my enemy say, "Pegge, it's time to take your medicine." I remember saying to the enemy, "Devil, you really messed up! Everything you have meant for evil against me, Jesus turned into a thing of beauty!" Jesus changed years of my pain and suffering into thirty years of time and training with God! And, what the Son sets free is free indeed." HALLELUJAH! I knew that everything I had lost during those thirty years would be compensated through the kingdom of heaven here on the earth. **The accident did not allow me to reach my dreams, but it allowed me to reach my calling,** which is above and beyond what I could ever think or imagine. As I spent my time with God, it no longer mattered whether I was going to be a farmer or a fisherman; what mattered the most was that He and I were going to bring souls to the Father. I wanted to live as Jesus Christ lived with His eyes and heart united to the Father, even as He was in the flesh, bringing the kingdom of heaven to the earth. God had heard the cries of the Israelites in Egypt, and He still hears our cries! I was one of those people. Jesus also heard our cries and was to "Go!" Go and reconnect our people in union with Us as it was before the fall of man. How could I have realized the truth of His glorious resurrection unless I was walking in "newness of life" (Romans 6:4)? The dark cloud of the enemy, the world, the flesh, and the devil were all placed under my feet!

Prayer:

Father, How proud I am that my Dad is the Ancient of Days! How blessed am I, and how bright is my future with You! Your Holy Spirit knows everything about You, Father. He knows what You think, how You act, Your heart, soul, and emotions. The Holy Spirit equipped Jesus through His completed mission on earth. His mission and my mission are not about reputation but character, bringing Your image and likeness to the earth. The Holy Spirit knows everything about us! The Holy Spirit is our witness on this earth to all of the miracles, signs, and wonders of Your love for us! Yet Your Holy Spirit, the third Person of the Godhead, is now living inside of me! How can we contain such wonder! You are not meant to be contained, just as I was not meant to be held in a body of pain. Jesus didn't look for a miracle to avoid the cross. He trusted You!

If you need a ministry to stand in faith for you, please contact us: Jesustodayministries.org

Prayer Points

We can read the Bible forever, but when we ask the Holy Spirit to show us what He wants us to see, life enters from the kingdom within to the manifestation without. What are you believing God for?

Jesus had faith that the Holy Spirit would resurrect Him from the tomb. Do you?

Jesus has placed all of our enemies under His feet. Do not go by what you see or hear but stand with Him in the Words of Life!

Jesus understands all you are going through. God's power is within you. We give to God our wounds, our tombs, everything we find ourselves dwelling with that are not alive in God. Let Jesus be Lord over it all.

Whose report will you believe?

If you need a ministry to stand in faith for you, please contact us: Jesustodayministries.org

Watch the miracles and testimonies on YouTube: Pegge Golden

Zoom Meetings/Training: jesustodayministries1@gmail.com

Chapter 9: The Overcomer

Chapter 9: The Overcomer

What a memorable ride home from the meeting! One of the girls was still being delivered, and I continued praying for her as I drove. This was the young girl I asked God to set free, and I believed God had answered my prayers for her. I loved watching all the different ways God intervenes in our lives, and each is as unique as we are. For months God had been healing her soul from a lifetime of suffering, and still more was being released. She was a chronic smoker, but after the meeting, she no longer had the desire to smoke. Halfway home, I stopped driving to switch over. I was so overcome with my encounter with Him, so excited for my healing but now wanted to rest and give Him all my attention. When I got in the back seat, the girl said she "wanted to try and see if she could smoke." She got out of the car but quickly came back. She said she tried, but the smoke would not go into her nose or mouth. She threw her cigarettes away.

When she got out of the car, she accidentally knocked my eyeglass case onto the ground. It had my driving glasses and my favorite sunglasses. She said she heard something fall when she got out, but it was dark, and she couldn't see. I asked the Lord to return my sunglasses and that I didn't care about my driving glasses. I released the angels on the assignment. We headed to our friend's home where we had gathered to drive to the meeting. When I opened my car door, my sunglasses were sitting on the passenger seat. Everyone saw me driving to the meeting with the very same glasses on, so we were praising God in my friend's driveway. As I headed home alone with God in my car, I could sense His sweet presence. I could feel no pain, and it was so "NEW!" The body that once held me captive was now restored! I had forgotten what it was like to live without pain. **"God, how can I thank YOU?"**

I slept through the entire night! When I opened my eyes in the morning, I raised my arms because I could, and said, **"YOU HEALED me, LORD! I knew You would!"** Even my shoulder was healed. I could feel the victory of His scars in a divine moment where I could sense every part of me in agreement with God; Who He is and What He said. I was overcome with the reality of what I remembered because I could! I began to journal, and I asked the Lord what He had done in me? I began writing His answer and speaking praises to God from my heart. The Holy Spirit still wanted to finish answering me, but I was so overcome with God's glory and His love that I was overflowing with thanksgiving. I was interrupted by the Holy Spirit, Who remained present with me in fire, and more fire was being released into my life. God was still not done, and His presence was heavy. He had released "His tree" into my life, and this was exactly how I felt, as if a tree was growing up into my spine and new muscles branching off from it.

I continued to write in my journal, and my healing was confirmed.

Being healed wasn't the end of the miracle, but just the beginning!

Then the Lord showed me something that looked like a "black film." I didn't understand the meaning at first, but then I realized that the "black film" was the adhesions. Hallelujah! I jumped from my bed and danced in the pure joy of heaven on earth! I spent the next week rejoicing. Weeks later, my glass case with my driving glasses was found in the back seat of my other friend's car. I kept telling all of them to watch for my glasses because I knew they were coming back to me. God wanted me to believe for the impossible, and He put those glasses in her car that never went to the meeting. Because of what I went through, so much of me was transformed, and this was the miracle itself! God conquered me and revealed His identity through my spirit, soul, body, mind, heart and strength! He LITERALLY changed my life! We agreed as one, and as I was yielding to Him, God taught me not to put limits on Him. My heavenly Father also taught me not to be satisfied or accept a partial victory!

So I began to seek the Lord as to what He meant by "full-time ministry." When I was just a little girl, I had a supernatural experience with God. It was a vision with the word "Union," and this word seemed etched upon my heart. As a child, I was given the understanding that when Jesus returned to heaven after His resurrection, He gave us authority to live like the redeemed or like Adam and Eve were living in the garden before the fall. The best part was that we can live like that in God right now and never had to wait for heaven! This vision remained alive in me like a seed that continued to grow with me throughout my life. As a young adult, a prophet gave a word that God was going to use people to "throw out a line and bring in a catch." I never forgot this prophecy, and I envisioned a fishing line going out and a net of fish coming in. I knew this word was for me from God. Amazingly, throughout all the damage from the accident and even decades-old, I never forgot these two experiences. On my bed of affliction, I experienced many visions, and as God brought His word to life in me, I continued watching how Jesus ministered, knowing He healed them all. The Holy Spirit would bring to my remembrance the gospel stories, the visions, and the prophetic words—but it wasn't until after my healing that the seed of "union" and the "online catch" were all connected to the future "full-time ministry."

When the prophetic word was released, I could not imagine how God could use the Internet as a ministry tool for His harvest, but now, thirty years later, the Internet was part of my own healing. From my vision as a child, what I knew without a doubt was what Jesus obtained for each of us through His atonement. For thirty years, I struggled to find the disconnect of why I wasn't manifesting my healing—and not just healing, because we were given dominion of the whole earth! Everything Jesus did with the early church was supposed to be happening right now and with even greater manifestation! The thing I remembered most from all the Bible stories was Jesus' heart for His people, and I knew that love came through obedience with the Father.

I had to learn to live over again.

I used to wonder what it was like to be a disciple of Jesus or imagine what Peter or John experienced as they walked with Jesus surrounded by people who were crying, confused, lonely, or outside of religious law. I wondered how often the disciples were tired, hungry, missed their families, or if they became frustrated in the crowds of demonized, incurable, hungry, and broken people. And, as this was their training ground, I imagined it was overwhelming until they would see Jesus weep out of His love for us. I thought of all who were homebound, and now that I was healed, what was my new role? I had so often thought of the man in the Bible who could not move, yet his friends lowered him on a stretcher through the roof so Jesus could pray for him. What faith these friends had to not be deterred from their mission with the vast crowds surrounding Jesus. Would I be like these friends to stand in strong faith for the afflicted? Would I serve the people of God with Jesus and His helpers? I had already been counseling face-to-face but wondered if my "full-time ministry" could be counseling online or by phone with Jesus healing all.

After hearing my testimony, people became so excited and hopeful that I could feel a cloud of faith surrounding us! The next week that same minister was doing another meeting a couple of states away from us, so we all decided to go. Again, we had the biggest van we could rent, and it was full. I could sense the enemy as soon as we crossed the state border. It rained so hard that we could barely see, but that just made us pray harder. I learned that if the enemy comes this strong against us, it is because he knows something amazing is about to happen—and not in his favor. The arguing in the van reached a new level, so I reminded the devil that he was losing his grip on everyone who came with us, and not only them but their families too. Prayer taught me to shoot Scripture like a gun, and I had wide sights on that evil kingdom. Before we left, I heard the Lord say that He wanted me "to help His minister." I had no details, but I figured I would be praying for this ministry and praying for what God was birthing in me. With everything coming against us getting to the meeting, I found such comfort remembering that the prayer team there was praying for our safe arrival and asked God to increase my faith.

When I was getting ready for the trip, I brought a change of clothes and planned on doing my hair and makeup when we arrived. We had scheduled to arrive two hours early to get to our hotel and grab a bite to eat before the meeting. The thunderstorm was severe, and all of a sudden, everyone's phone batteries were dead. Even when they plugged their phones in, there was no signal or charge. My phone was working except for the GPS. We were lost! When we arrived, the parking lot was so full that we parked in the grass. We walked in the dark through the mud in the downpour!

I had to learn to maintain my healing and deliverance.

We found seats in the last row, and there we sat, soaking wet. The meeting had begun, and the young children we brought with us were restless and noisy. The people were glancing at us, and I can only imagine how we looked! The minister started talking about the girl named "Pegge" who was healed the week before, and I raised my hand. The meeting was in a building that looked like a small warehouse, and the lighting was not good in the back, but he saw a hand raised and asked if it was me. He wanted me to come up to the front and give my testimony. The thought of how I looked while being on camera could not touch the joy of honoring my Father with my testimony of His faithfulness! **Jesus knew what I had gone through to get to this meeting because He went through it with me and my testimony was all for Him!** I honestly thought my future ministry was sharing my testimony for all that He had done for the rest of my life!

After the message, the minister asked if I would be his prayer helper. I agreed, and the Holy Spirit covered me with instructions and the ministry He was talking to me about was birthed. This was not Dad talking to His girl. This was the pure power of God! He was teaching me ministry with specifics! God was instructing me how to pray while staying out of His way! As the meeting was winding down, the minister asked me to pray for people. The Holy Spirit gave me strict instructions to watch and listen to Him and not focus on the person because He knew everything about the person, so I didn't need to. I obeyed the process, and this is how the Holy Spirit continues to minister every day since.

Within the next two weeks, because of my testimony, I had received offers to come and do meetings in Ohio and North Carolina. I was walking on blind faith! The good news was that I knew I could not heal anyone, and this was my opening message in the church of Ohio. After all I experienced, I was overcome by the fact that in a matter of weeks, I went from being healed to ministering as Jesus sets His people free! Everything God had shown me during those thirty years of suffering and learning, He was now doing! I was so humbled by His love, realizing that He birthed this ministry during my suffering, watching how He healed me.

Being healed wasn't the end of the miracle, but just the beginning!

I had to learn to live over again. I had to learn to maintain my healing and deliverance. I had to learn to follow God in this new season and live in His strength. I told my doctors that Jesus healed me, but they did not believe in miracles. I made an appointment with my doctor to tell him I no longer wanted all the pills. I had no withdrawal symptoms after the meeting, and the weight was coming off of me. When he saw how much weight I had lost, he said, "You must be in love." It took a couple of more visits for him to see that I meant it. He said I was his first patient to remove their prescriptions! He was so blessed by my testimony that he called all the nurses into my room, and I gave God all the glory.

During the next meeting in North Carolina, God did many miraculous works again. After the meeting, a woman who was touched by God offered me a free massage. She said she wanted to feel my muscles to confirm they were healed, and as a massage therapist, she was so amazed at the condition of my muscles that she flew to the next miracle meeting! My testimony and seeing God move in power charged her faith by restoring her hope in Jesus!

God expanding the ministry was new to me but not to the devil. I was also a single woman depending on the covering of my pastors, intercessors, and those He placed around me. I had gone from being homebound with poor memory, few friends, and days almost indistinguishable from one another to traveling around and staying with people I had just met. My comfort was only found knowing God had total control and I was cooperating with Him. I had to learn to keep fear under my feet and wisdom as my guide, for He is my Protector. I would seek counsel from those who would tell me the truth, to advise me of anything they saw that I did not. My reflection of Him to each and every person I met was of utmost importance to me as I saw my suffering in each of them. I also began working online with the minister. He advised me to build a website to put up the testimonies of all those I prayed for Online who God had miraculously healed. I didn't know how to build a website, but I knew God's grace is sufficient. I didn't have much money either and was totally dependent on God for provision! This was His ministry, and I counted on His administration and guidance.

I had to take responsibility for the care of my temple because I saw how the enemy once snared it. This process of overcoming could never be taken lightly ever again! My being could only remain in perfect health under the authority and promises of Jesus Christ. If I felt any kind of pain in my body, I was like a blazing soldier taking it captive and commanding it out. I had to watch the belief of those around me, including all I was listening to or looking at. I had to watch the enemy too. I knew he would test my faith, trying to take back the ground in me that he lost! I had to pay attention to anything my flesh was agreeing with. If the enemy didn't stop after tempting Jesus, how could I ever again think he would stop regarding me?

One day about three months after my healing, out of nowhere, pain covered my body. The miracle-working power of God had been so complete that I had forgotten what that pain felt like. The enemy made an attempt to deliver "a gift" to me. "Well, devil, I forgot what that pain felt like, and now that you have reminded me, I am going to pray even more eagerly for myself and others." I bound every symptom of pain, giving it back to the enemy by the authority of Jesus Christ in me. Immediately, as fast as the pain came, it left my body! I was to guard my temple from within my spirit life with God.

Jesus meant it when He warned us to be sober and awake and to keep watch! I learned to guard who I am in Christ because I had a lack of understanding and could so easily drift off the path back into the world system when I didn't. I saw how easy habits are created through drifting that will not only change my path but cover me in the wrong garments of thought, word, and deed. I know my mind is a force to be reckoned with that wants to have control, but I learned how to take authority over my mind with the mind of Christ. I learned to take any thought, word, or action that did not line up with the ways of God to the fires of yielding. The Bible tells us that if possible, even the elect will be deceived in the end times. I didn't know how deceived I was until my idea of life no longer functioned.

These were the hardest and most profitable lessons, and God used what the enemy meant for evil to restore my life and unveil my calling and destiny. Do I still make mistakes? Yes, but the Lord's rod and staff are here to comfort me because I trust Him to see what I do not. I now understand that discipline is a gift from God. I cannot be healed and then return to my old way of operating. I have to continue to put off the old and mature in the new man. I knew God but had lost that deep hunger. I used to crave God so badly that I got up in the dark to pray and seek Him. I had to watch my level of hunger and thirst for God's Word, my prayer time, and fasting. Jesus fed me daily, and His living waters filled me with His movement. My passion for God was rekindled, and my life was resurrected from the dead. I am no longer a pillar of salt, but available for God to move through. I have no more reputation or agenda. I submit, stripped of all. I had been crushed down, broken but not destroyed. Through all the miracles my prayer life being resurrected with God with my tears flowing for others meant the most to me.

I made a vow with God when I gave Him my life, but I took the warnings for granted. The Bible showed me repeatedly how when there was peace in the land, the people became slack and stopped depending on God. Times of peace now mean extra thankfulness as I cling to God, praying and sowing into my tomorrow as well as my family. I was never created to follow the traditions of men but by Jesus' example. The enemy wanted to overtake me, but my Savior wanted me to overcome. All the world had to offer could not help me— Jesus has always been the Answer!

God loves us even when we have forgotten our identity in Him, but it's time to wake up to who we are in Christ and all that He has accomplished for us. Are you ready if a tragedy comes to your home or neighborhood? Are you praying every day for your tomorrow and that of your family and friends? God said that He would transform us, regenerate us, and bring us to maturity—but He doesn't do this without us. We cannot take dominion if we allow our emotions, desires, strength, time, past, religion, or even our own hearts to defeat us. I needed a breakthrough, and Holy Spirit broke through as man, the world, the television could not save me. God restored His fire in me that made me burn for Him as when I was first saved. My life had to match my words, which had to line up with my thoughts and actions to Jesus.

We overcome in our relationship of union with God as we work together with the Blood of Jesus and the word of our testimony. I thank God for Jesus' prayer life! The enemy knows that our free will has a choice to make every single day. And God has prepared a table for us in the presence of our enemies. I am His sheep and His guest. He allows the enemy to see Him protecting us, but I wanted all sin an self out of the way of God's divine plan for me. And for us in Christ, God has already overcome, and with the Holy Spirit living within us, nothing is impossible for us who believe Him! Each of us has a destiny in Christ now! Why He healed others and not me drove me into the wilderness with Him for my answers. I could see division within myself and why God wanted me to love Him with my whole heart, soul, mind, and strength; in unity, we are not drifting away, and with God, those who surround us are loved with His love and His manifested presence!

We have all been told to read the Word, to stay in the Word, and that life is found in the Word of God, but do we really believe this? If the Word is life to a believer, how serious are we about our life? The Holy Spirit is our Teacher, or do we look to others? And if we sincerely believe that God is living right within us, then why do we treat Him as if He isn't there? And when we know God lives within us, what should be the change we experience, and what are our neighbors experiencing because of His life in us?

I went from wanting a miracle back to walking with Him. As He healed others, He was burning the dross, removing the junk from my life. He was showing me to watch in spirit when nothing happens on the earth. My miracle was that I would never leave Him again. Only Jesus could carry me through all the suffering and disappointment I went through, and Jesus cares for the rest of us. For Him, it was all about us, but for us, it is only about Him. My suffering was as personal as it gets with God, but my healing was all about others. I want God's will to live and His desires to be met. I have His courage, His strength, His promises, and the Bread of Life sustained me.

Most all of us have read the stories, but do we understand that we are citizens of heaven now and that our life depends on His word every single day—not just the ink on paper, but the person of God. I did not! I do not want anyone to go through what I did, and neither does Jesus as He went through it all for us. When I could not function, the Holy Spirit enabled me to overcome by helping me remember the stories, teachings, the truth, and the promises of God. I believe the Lord showed me that many of us lose hope while waiting for Jesus to show up and just heal us. Some want Jesus to come and heal them so they can return to their old way of living. Some want deliverance, which is available, but will they become serious students of the faith to maintain the enemy from returning? Are we willing to work the miracle to the healing of our souls? We have missed the point—Jesus is waiting on us! I used to wonder how long it would take Jesus and the early church to show up for each of us to do a miracle healing service. Would we give our all to attend that meeting, and would we return to thank Him and testify of all He has done in each of our lives! He has shown up for each of us. For those of us who are healed, we are to stand in His faith as He sets those around us free. For those still waiting, how will you respond? Refuse to doubt, knowing that God's power has overcome no matter what any other voices have to say. Pray in the power of the Holy Spirit, knowing that God's life-breath is within you! Those who have gone before us have prayed for this generation. We need to take time to pray for the generations to come after us.

I received enlightenment from the Holy Spirit about the men who stood to carry the paralytic man (Mark 2:1-12). They went and brought the man who could not walk to Jesus.

They knew how to reach the person of God. Who knows if these men had also received healing? I just know that when a person receives healing through their encounter with Jesus the only thing left after that is to bring others to Him. Jesus told us that we will do greater works than He did because we do them together. I love watching the supernatural power of God with miracles, signs, and wonders. I love the Word, the meetings, and His people but I want God most of all, and my daily time in Him is my treasure! Every day is like drilling for oil! There are so many levels to each of us, and the Holy Spirit is the drill! The deeper the drill, the more I realize with a healthy fear of God that He places His "super" in my "natural" and reveals the kingdom of heaven within me. I believe one of the greatest lessons I learned from all of this was to focus on finishing well and spending each day expanding the kingdom here on earth!

God doesn't make us sick nor does He use sickness to test our faith. He already knows if we have faith or not. He already knows He paid the price for our healing, salvation, deliverance, and every blessing and promise He has made available for us. These promises are for those who believe Him. He wants us to move in the benefits of His atonement as though we have received Him and believed Him. I remembered all the dreams and thoughts I had of all God would do with me, but it was never me who would do it. All glory belongs to God! Oh, the joys of surrender to His majesty, letting go of my futile thinking. God would not be God if I could figure Him out! Letting go of how we think He should behave showed me how I was behaving. In my brokenness, I glimpsed His love and I want to devote my time to the love God has for me and return my love for Him.

We are growing and maturing in faith. Things don't usually come easy for the believer, but the deeper we go with God, the more He is increasing us with Himself. Faith grows with each question of "Will we trust Him?" and "Will we do our part to believe He is able?" The Word has everything we need to know while we walk this earth. Some would rather complain than read it. Some would rather ignore the Holy Spirit. Some would feel they don't have to pray and relate with God because Jesus is praying for us. God is with us to overcome the world, the flesh, and the devil every single day of our lives. He sees us, knows us, and is waiting for our response to do life with Him! Responding in union with the Holy Spirit brought me out of my disability, and I know He will sustain me through every trial I encounter. The Lord has overcome everything! Hallelujah! It took all of this to open my eyes to see how truly blessed I am because God is my God and I am His child. I had taken my eyes off of the vision of God for the world, but through all I suffered, it was revived. His vision was never the sick and diseased waiting to go to heaven. His vision was for everyone to realize that He is still walking the earth with us and through us. This can only happen as we, His disciple, learn from the Teacher.

I will not allow the world to tell me that I am too old for my ministry calling. Abraham didn't even start his God-job until he was seventy-five. Sarah had Isaac at ninety years old. I speak over my life that my latter years will be greater than the first, and I will fulfill every adventure God wants to have with me. I do not want to stand in the very presence of Almighty God and be missing my "leeks and onions." **I am going forward in Him!** He died for me to be made whole now, and I want all He paid the price for me to have! My recovery began the day I was born—and so did my transformation. As I suffered, I learned that every miracle of my salvation is dwelling within me, and God has continued to prepare me, like a bride, for the day I meet His Son! I want to be a beautiful bride. I may have wrinkles on the outside, but He took my scars on the inside. I may have age spots, but He and I are conquering my mountains together.

Since my healing and for the last two years, I have continued to watch God be God as He unfolds His "full-time ministry." The Holy Spirit brings His people to me and He "prepares a table before us." He allows me to pray with others whose bodies have been hit with the fiery darts of the enemy, afflicting their bodies as the fires torment their minds. I pray with them in their homes over a phone, social media, or Zoom, and God is faithful. I travel and do ministry meetings. I have prayed with people using an online translator, and God has faithfully healed them. There truly is no distance or limits for God. There are testimonies of God healing or delivering someone as soon as I schedule their meeting time! God's counsel always amazes the client and me. I cannot even count how many times when I just opened a session with a new client by prayer or just simply said in Jesus' name, and He was already done. It was like He couldn't wait any longer! This is the love God has for each of us. This is the God I knew as a little girl before life got in the way. How many nights would I go to bed and say, "God, I don't see how You can out do what You did today." But He always does! I am a believer, just like you, greatly honored to serve the One who came to serve me! I love my Boss and my job!

Prayer:

Father, this book is Your testimony of what You did in my life, and I am Your witness. I am watching You build Your army! As You encounter Your people, they also do the same. I watch how You bring people for prayer, salvation, and deliverance and I am honored to love Your people with You. And when You release Your miracles, they do not stop. You have me contact those You healed months later to see if they are maintaining their healing and deliverance. Some need more of You. Some deliver slower than others. Some are healed instantly, while some are healed later. Some suffer long but their prayers have brought healing to many. Some will testify on YouTube, while others have their video written upon their hearts and memory banks. Some will want prayer for a child, but You will heal the mom, then the dad, then the sister and then the child! Some will want a new limb, but You give them a new heart and a ministry to those who are handicapped. The people who were most demonized are now doing deliverance ministry. Some die in faith and enter into Your open waiting arms. Your leaders persevere at all costs, even when they see little change. You know loss more than we can imagine, as You watched Your Son die to recover all. May we each respond to Your kingdom work on the earth. May we each continue Your testimony as Your Bible continues to be written with us. We will never know how many You have touched by what we go through, our prayers, and ministry until we are gathered to You and we hear Your testimony of us. I ask You to awaken each of us and restore our hunger and thirst for You. You are limitless! Holy Spirit, we want to be vessels of honor for You! You harvest through every prayer we speak. Thank You, Father, because You are awakening us and reviving us to live in union with You now! May Your gift of Jesus be multiplied as we carry You to each person we meet, in Jesus' beautiful name! Amen!

Prayer Points

Everything we go through is part of our future ministry. Mine was birthed during my suffering. I see my suffering in the affliction of others God brings before me.

Your life is not mundane—you are planning your wedding with the Lord!

The kingdom of heaven is alive within you. Enjoy your time NOW with your King.

Are you teaching the young about Jesus?

Will you pray for the next generation?

Drop us an email and let us know what you think of the book: jesustodayministries1@gmail.org

If you would like prayer please send in a prayer request: jesustodayministries.org/prayer-by-appointment/

If you would like to schedule a meeting: jesustodayministries.org/meetings/

If you would to financially partner with this ministry: jesustodayministries.org/donations/

Prayer of Salvation

Prayer of Salvation

If you have never asked Jesus to be the Lord and Savior of your life, let today be your choice to begin a life spent eternally with the One true God who loves you! Even if you are unable to receive His love, let Him find the way into your heart:

Father, I thank You for sending Jesus to come in the flesh as God and man to dwell with us, to relate with us, to die for us, and to shed His Blood to pay the price for my sin. I thank You, Father, that as Jesus was raised from the dead, the veil of the temple was torn, removing all that got in the way of our relationship. Jesus, I believe You died for me, shed Your Blood on the cross, and resurrected to prepare a place for me, and if all that wasn't enough, You pray for me day and night. I am sorry for allowing sin to strain our relationship. Wash me clean with Your precious Blood. Free me from the sins of my ancestors and any curses that I am continuing on in my bloodlines.

Awaken me, God, as you fill me with your precious Holy Spirit, the same Holy Spirit that dwelled with Jesus, filled Him, and resurrected Him from the dead. Uncover every deception in me! Open my spiritual life to You and write my name in Your Lamb's Book of Life! I want

You to overtake me and make us one as You and the Father are One. Thank You for restoring me and taking me from eternal darkness into Your eternal kingdom, where I dwell with You now and forever. I want to unite my desires with Yours, my spirit with Yours, my soul with Yours, and my body with Yours. For now and as long as I continue to abide in You, it will be in You that I live and move and have my being!

Note: If you have prayed this prayer for the first time or if it is your first time praying with understanding, please contact jesustodayministries.org as we would welcome the chance to celebrate with you as all of heaven! This prayer is your new beginning, but the walk through life is to be with God as our Head and us as His body. We need God, and we need each other, and we need to remain in the fellowship of the believers. Amen!

About the Author

Pegge Golden is the Founder of Jesus Today Ministries, where her mission is for all to know that Jesus is with us to heal, save, deliver and restore. She went to school at Assumption College in Massachusetts and Oral Roberts University and has a MA from Christian Leadership University. She is a pastor with a master's in Christian counseling. Pegge shares her testimony of hope in the States and abroad. She has been teaching young people the Word of God for over fifty years and does online Bible Studies, miracle meetings, and counseling for deliverance and healing. When not ministering, Pegge enjoys spending time with her family and grandchildren and is an avid gardener.

We invite you to attend our Online or in-person Miracle Meetings.

For prayer, itinerary, donations, and resources visit:
www.jesustodayministries.org

For teachings and testimonies:
YouTube Pegge Golden

CPSIA information can be obtained
at www.ICGtesting.com
Printed in the USA
BVHW052159220623
666253BV00016B/988

9 781737 635604